DO WE REALLY REAP
WHAT WE SOW?

MARK HERRINGSHAW

MINNEAPOLIS, MINNESOTA

Art direction by Paul Higdon
Cover design by The Design Works Group, Connie Gabbert

Published by Bethany House Publishers
11400 Hampshire Avenue South
Bloomington, Minnesota 55438

Bethany House Publishers is a division of
Baker Publishing Group, Grand Rapids, Michigan.

Printed in the United States of America

Library of Congress Cataloging-in-Publication Data

Herringshaw, Mark.
    The karma of Jesus : do we really reap what we sow? / Mark Herringshaw.
        p.   cm.
    Includes bibliographical references.
    Summary: "A pastor explores the spiritual concept of karma to explain grace, Christian atonement, and the life of Christ"—Provided by publisher.
    ISBN 978-0-7642-0734-1 (pbk. : alk. paper)   1. Christianity and other religions. 2. Karma   3. Christianity—21st century.   I. Title.
    BR127.H487   2009
    216.2'4—dc22
                                                                                            2009025240

To my father

and his memory

BOOKS "HAPPEN" FOR A REASON

Those who wish to demonstrate that "design" in the world indicates a Designer sometimes compare the odds of order appearing accidently to a monkey randomly pounding on a keyboard and producing *War and Peace.* I don't know if this argument proves God, but I can vouch from experience: Books, at least, do not happen by accident.

Nor do they happen alone. Behind all my early morning/late night stints, a band of partners have stood challenging, encouraging, correcting, demanding, interceding, and rescuing me. Without them I would have been nothing more than a chimp playing hunt and peck.

First, to Beth Jusino, my agent, and also to the entire Alive Communications team: Beth, you recognized the potential of this idea before I did. Your guidance helped hone not only its development but the fabulous partnership we formed with Bethany and Baker. You will be missed; but you need never miss God's first best, no matter what. . . .

To Kyle Duncan at Bethany House: You caught the vision and cut a safe path for what could have been a "dangerous" project. Thanks for your courage, faith, and contagious joy.

To Jeff Braun: Thank you for your kinship. Once the dust settles we'll grab lunch and follow those rabbit trail conversations we've never had time to pursue. Thank you for your gentle honesty about what didn't work, your encouragement of what did, and your challenge for what could become better.

To the entire Bethany House team: Tim Peterson, Jim Hart, Brett Benson, and Carra Carr, who have delivered this book into the hands that matter; Paul Higdon, who gave the idea a visual presence; and Nancy Renich, who corrected my mistakes of oversight and ignorance. Thank you all.

To those—some knowingly, some unknowingly—who contributed to the ideas and stories in this book: Please know that imitation is the sweetest form of flattery.

I was fortunate to have several early readers who invested time reviewing and advising me on some or all of the manuscript: Steve Whiting, Marcus Haug, Bob Cottingham, Bill Sims, and Jennifer Schuchmann. You helped me say what I mean, and understand what I was saying.

To my children, Emily, Elizabeth, Matthew, and Michael Herringshaw, my delight, pride, and hope! You were patient and supportive to the (sometimes) bitter end. I trust that what I've completed here honors you and speaks to you and to your generation.

To Jill, my wife: If I had to count on Karma for my reward, I'd be in trouble. You are my image and model of grace, both in your heart for God and in your tender mercies toward me.

To all the laborers backstage: printers, loading dock supervisors, truckers, book buyers, bookstore owners, sales people, janitors (who mop the floors when customers spill latte in the store), critics (I speak in faith), bloggers, and librarians. I don't know your names, but thank you. Books like this happen in part because good people do their jobs well without much recognition.

To my friends and family who prayed for me when I needed most the guidance, protection, wisdom, and strength of God: Thank you most of all! May this work honor the One who is the Cause behind all good effects!

Mark
St. Paul, Minnesota

WITHIN

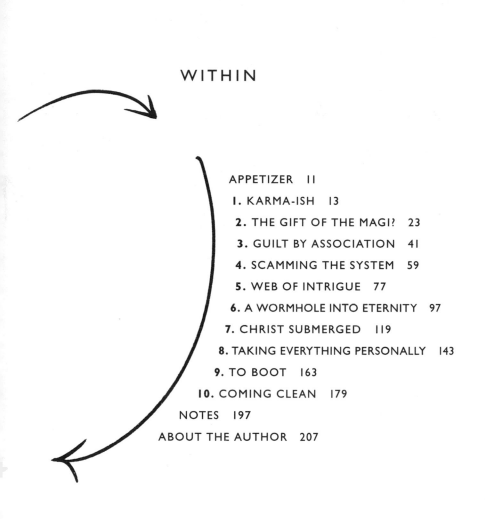

APPETIZER

Chili pepper, absolutely.

Chocolate, most definitely.

But together?

You wouldn't think so, but try it. A dash of cayenne on a dark chocolate truffle . . . ambrosia.

Sometimes things that seem opposites actually belong together.

Take Karma and Jesus . . .

I know. How can these two words stand with integrity in the title on the cover of the same book? It's counter-intuitive, I agree.

I've heard reactions and ridicule from both sides. Those who adhere to the philosophy of Karma see the name *Jesus* attached and roll their eyes. "Another attempt to hobble this clean and clear truth with an arcane religion. No thanks."

From across the abyss, loyal followers of Jesus boil over at the suggestion that their master's simple message and pure life could be so contaminated. I've heard them mutter under their breath the dreaded *H* word—*"Heresy!"*

Well, chili aficionados and chocolate connoisseurs, Karma adherents and Jesus followers, unite. Let me here suggest a recipe, surprising as it is simple, that compromises neither Karma nor Jesus and in fact enhances our understanding of them both.

Taste and see . . .

KARMA-ISH

"Do things happen for a reason?"

The question stopped me mid-sentence. I had been speaking to a full room, and for the first ten minutes all eyes had been on me. Suddenly every head turned toward the voice.

I shot a glance in the same direction. *Great, a heckler,* I thought. *I don't need this tonight.*

The man's wispy words hung in the air like a fog. Yet he had spoken clearly enough so that all 150 people present could hear him.

I stepped downstage, glanced at my shoes, then up again and instantly locked eyes with a young man in his early twenties seated seven rows back: my inquisitor.

"Do things happen for a reason?" he asked me again.

Sincere? Confused? Or worse? I studied him and weighed my options. Typically, people listen quietly when I speak publicly, often too quietly—I live in St. Paul and our crowds are "Minnesota nice." If they have questions, they come up after the event and we talk one-on-one. This guy didn't know the rules of engagement.

After a swig from my water bottle, I cleared my throat and started searching for a way to segue back to my talk. "Sure . . ." I conceded. "If you mean is there a reason for our lives. Yeah, I believe there's a reason, a big story. I believe God is the storyteller and we're the characters." *Smug, perhaps, but justified,* I told myself. I panned my notes for a good reentry point before he could call me out for ducking his question with a cliché.

Even as I began speaking again, his question swam like Muzak in the elevator shafts of my brain. *Do things happen for a reason?* He'd hit a nerve.

Of course things happen for a reason. My fingers were still tingling *because* that afternoon I had been outside without warm gloves. Warm gloves mattered *because* the windchill that Saturday in February had fallen to 25 degrees below zero. I'd been outside *because* my car battery had died and I needed a jump. My battery had died *because* I'd forgotten to turn off my headlights. I'd forgotten to turn off my headlights *because* . . . *Because* makes way for an explanation—a "why"—a reason.

I'd played this discovery game all my life, since I first stuck green peas up my nose to see if they'd come out my ear and dropped salamanders into jars of scalding water and flushed toothbrushes down the toilet just to see what would happen.

Most of us gain common sense through childish experimentation. It all began in our first weeks on the planet, when we found that our hands could move as we told them to move. Eventually we could reach and touch and grab and gnaw the fur off a teddy bear. We learned that crashing our head against the side of the crib hurt (we stopped that) and that our screams could muster a response from big soft arms that would bring us comfort (so we did more of that). We learned cause and effect, and we've never stopped learning and turning our knowledge, whenever possible, to our advantage.

Whenever possible. Sometimes learning a cause behind an effect can't bring any advantage. It just brings bad news, period. I'd discovered this the hard way a few days earlier.

My sister's phone call that Tuesday morning woke me early. My father was unconscious and on his way in an ambulance to the hospital. He'd awakened before sunrise with a piercing headache, said a few stumbling words to my mother, and then quickly and quietly fell into a coma.

Forty minutes after I heard the news, I stood awkwardly beside my father's bed in the critical care unit of United Hospital, trying to sort out what it meant, what it would mean, and why it had happened. Things happen for a reason, don't they?

The immediate reason showed plainly on the X-rays. A blood vessel in the right hemisphere had ruptured, flooding my father's brain tissue. The attending physician spoke kindly but plainly. "This kind of hemorrhage usually leads to a loss of quality of life. Treatment options are limited by Howard's other health concerns. Taking him off the blood thinner prescribed for his heart would help slow the hemorrhage but raise the risk of a heart attack."

"Did the blood thinner cause the hemorrhage?" my sister DeAnn asked directly.

The doctor studied her clipboard, then looked up and spoke eye to eye with DeAnn. "We never say 'cause' in a case like this. His condition came from a complicated inter-relationship of conditions and events, which no one can piece together in a perfect fixed order. Small hemorrhages for someone Howard's age are common. And he needed the blood thinner as a hedge against heart disease. . . . And I'm sure the cardiologist explained the potential side effects . . . one of which is . . . complicating this kind of stroke. So we're always playing one danger off another. There is no one cause for an injury like this." She seemed resigned to ambiguity. I was not, and my heckler's question rubbed raw this wound of confusion.

Then just as I was regaining my rhetorical groove, he struck again.

"Does God forgive?" he asked.

The audience laughed. I smiled. The young man seemed earnest. A wave of confidence and relief flooded me. This felt like home-field advantage. I could deal with this question. I looked him in the eye again and began. "Well, I believe God forgives. That is foundational to our faith. I have experienced it. I think a lot of people around you here tonight would say they've experienced God's forgiveness." He nodded but didn't seem fully satisfied.

I moved on. A few minutes later he fired off another round. "Doesn't the Sublime One, the Buddha, suggest that there are many paths toward God?"

No laughter this time; I could see people squirming. A murmuring wave rolled across the room. "Sure," I said, without seeing exactly where I should head. "Many paths *toward* God, but only one leads *to* God." I looked around to see how my wordplay had impressed the spectators.

Evidently they weren't as awed as I had been myself. I shrugged, stepped back behind the podium, and continued my agenda.

Finally, at a particularly salient moment toward the end of my talk, the young man pulled out his trump card. "Why did Jesus die?"

I looked at him for the time it takes to pull in two or three deep breaths. *God help me,* I thought. "These are good questions, good in a place like this," I acknowledged, as much to the audience as to the young man. "But this probably isn't the best context for our personal conversation. Come up afterward and we can talk."

I finished, and the room emptied out, except for a few stragglers who hung in the wings hoping to eavesdrop on the pending encounter. To my surprise, the young man took the offer, walked toward me, introduced himself as Andrew, and sat in the front row. I sorted my papers, quickly greeted a few people, then pulled a chair around and sat facing him.

Andrew began his story. He'd grown up attending a Christian church. In high school he started using drugs. The drugs became an addiction. He eventually found freedom in a rehab program anchored in some form of New Age philosophy. His mother had brought him to hear me speak that evening, hoping he might reconnect with his spiritual roots.

Andrew talked freely. I listened, groping for some common language we could use to truly communicate.

"Just bad Karma, I guess—" Andrew added near the end of a thought I hadn't completely followed.

"What's that?" I cut in.

"Bad Karma," he said. "The stuff that happened to me must have been bad Karma."

"You believe in Karma?"

He looked quizzically at me. "Of course."

Karma. I sifted my memory bank for a quick cross-reference. And who should come to mind? Not Buddha meditating under a lotus tree, or Krishna lecturing Arjuna in the *Bhagavad Gita,* or Gandhi spinning yarn for his cotton smocks, or George Harrison holding a fistful of daisies, or Eckhart Tolle living in the "now," or the Dalai Lama smiling passively. No, when I first thought of *Karma,* Earl came to mind. Ah, the power of pop culture!

I don't watch much television, but when boredom overwhelmed me one Thursday night, I started flipping channels. The Twins baseball game was rained out, so I landed on a rerun of NBC's *My Name Is Earl* and laughed my way through an hour of Karmic evangelism. Backstory: Earl Hickey wins $100,000 on a scratch-off lottery ticket and dances in the street to celebrate. Then *wham!* Three seconds later he's sprawled on the pavement with tire tracks across his back and his ticket sailing off in the wind.

While recovering in the hospital, Earl reflects on his misery: a wife who cheated on him, money problems, dead-end jobs that usually ended with Earl punching his boss.

Then late one night Earl hears country singer Trace Adkins on Carson Daly's television show explain his philosophy. Adkins says he believes in Karma: that good comes when we do good; bad comes when we do bad. We can determine what happens in our lives by directing our choices. Adkins calls it "simple cause and effect: You get back whatever you give out."

This proves to be an Aha! moment for Earl. He compares Trace Adkins' life of fame, wealth, and the companionship of beautiful women with his trailer-court-trash world of petty crime and perpetual turmoil. Then and there Earl converts. He becomes a devotee to the law of Karma.

Earl acts on his convictions. He grabs a notepad and pen and begins to list all the nasty things he's ever done: stealing a car from a one-legged girl right after telling her he loved her, holding a garage sale while house-sitting for neighbors, peeing in the back of a cop car, fixing a high school football game . . .

Earl then sets out to redeem himself and repair his Karma. His strategy: Do a good deed to counter every bad one. It seems to work. The very day Earl starts his "new life," he finds his lost lottery ticket!

What happened as Earl worked his list provided a stream of ingenious story lines for the quirky, sometimes profound, comedy. The show also served up a primer of the pop version of Karma touted by the likes of Oprah, Marianne Williamson, Gary Zukav, Deepak Chopra, and Rhonda Byrne. Byrne's wildly popular book *The Secret* renames Karma "the law of attraction," calling it the singular most important principle in the world. This brand of Karma-lite comes complete with a side dish of American optimism, a faddish method to cowboy your way to success, and a promise that you can create your own destiny.

I looked at Andrew and tried to picture him playing Earl. I wondered too if he'd ever considered the darker side of his proposition or experienced the deep sadness—even despair—that sometimes emanates from the doctrine of Karma as it's expressed in the ancient religions of the East.

"So what does Karma mean to you?" I asked.

"Do good, good comes back," he said. "Screw up, trouble comes back."

"Does it work?"

"That's what I'm saying. I stole stuff to support my habit; I landed in court. I quit using; I landed a job. I started speaking with kindness; I have friends. I give away things; I get what I need. What goes around comes around. Things happen for a reason, and it seems like Karma runs the world."

"And by controlling Karma you control your own part of the world," I suggested.

Andrew shrugged but didn't respond.

I sat back and stared at the ceiling for a moment. I had to admit, Andrew's—and Earl's—shorthand version of the ancient, very intricate philosophy of Karma seemed to make simple, intuitive sense. I schedule my days, eat meals, save and spend money, and communicate with friends and family, assuming that outcomes flow predictably from my actions. I teach my children that good deeds pay for themselves. I've even caught myself imagining that the pint of blood I donate will buy me an extra day tacked on to the end of my life. At a gut level, I presume the universe will pay dividends on my investments and levy excise taxes on my conspicuous consumption. Was it coincidence when I cut in front of a senior citizen on the turnpike and five miles later blew a head gasket?

A list of Karma-ish proverbs I've used in everyday conversations rattled up to the surface of my mind:

- "For every action there is an equal and opposite reaction."
- "What goes around comes around."

- "We reap what we sow."
- "Waiting for the other shoe to drop."

Did I buy this? I may have forgotten most of the algebra I learned in school, but I still feel dissonance when two sides of my equations don't balance. When life flows too easily, I get suspicious and uneasy, half expecting trouble to follow. When things turn inexplicably miserable, I complain to the heavens for a reprieve, or at least a reasonable explanation: "Tell me what caused my father's stroke."

Perhaps this innate human passion for fairness and reason, as well as causes matching effects, makes Karma one of the oldest and easiest ideas in the world to believe, and why through its many and sometimes impossibly sophisticated forms it has popped up so many times throughout human history.

I looked at Andrew and saw in him an American digest of three thousand years of human speculation about how the world works.

"Is it that simple—Karma runs the world?" I asked.

"You have a better theory?" Andrew folded his arms and leaned back in the chair.

"Maybe I could agree if I could actually control life perfectly with my choices, as you say. Then it might be the best news ever. But Karma seems like physics done in space—great in theory, but then gravity sets in."

"It's working for me," he said flatly.

"I can only speak for myself," I said, thinking again of my father lying on a bed with tubes running in and out of his body. "Perfectly figuring out all the reasons for things seems hard enough, let alone trying to engineer those reasons. In my experience it always seems easier to screw up than to make things work just right."

He shrugged. "I can't think that way. For the first time I've got hope that I can make something of myself."

"A good life is a hard thing to hold together," I said.

Andrew ran his fingers through his hair as if to fend off my skepticism. Then he leaned forward. "So, why did Jesus die?"

THE GIFT OF THE MAGI?

I suspected Andrew wouldn't swallow a seminary explanation to his question, and he was too clever for a snow job. I wished my father had been there. He had a seminary education too, but he never talked it up. At the moment he couldn't have bantered with Andrew even if he'd wanted to. But banter wasn't his way. In fact, I'd never heard him dispute ideas. He'd listen to people's stories, ask a question, and wait. Then when the time seemed right, he'd just walk with them to Jesus. It happened probably two hundred times over his lifetime.

Andrew had asked me this Jesus question twice; it meant something to him, and I—not my father—was the one present and accounted for. Uncertain how to proceed, I retreated to noodling him more about his Karma comments.

"What do you know about the history of the Karma idea?" I asked.

He shrugged as if he couldn't care less, then added, "It's Hindu, Buddhist, and Greek too, I think." He paused to let me fill in the details.

I couldn't, not fully at least. I'd read about Karma. But when I tried to call up details, only bits and pieces broke loose from the floor of my mind. Debaters don't ask questions they can't answer themselves, but this was not a debate. I figured I would learn what I could from his explanations and go from there.

"What do *you* know about it?" Andrew asked, calling my bluff.

"Some," I admitted. I then kept talking and thinking out loud until I had strung together a rambling and rough (emphasis on *rough*) outline of the philosophy known to most of the world as *Karma*.

That was then; this is now.

Writing a book that looks back on an actual conversation offers a tantalizing opportunity to editorialize and supplement elements I should have added at the time but didn't. I'll resist.

Instead, with a stack of good books beside me and a cable connecting me to more information than I know what to do with, I'll remove the quotation marks and relay the story as straight as I can, outside the "Andrew" context.

On one particular evening sometime before midnight, in June of the year we call 2 BCE, a bearded man in a priest's tunic and a boy in his teens climbed an observation tower near the outskirts of the ancient city of Babylon. The man carried several scrolls and the boy some candles and an armload of geometric instruments used for plotting the movement of the planets against the backdrop of fixed stars. The man was a magus and the boy, his student.

They made this climb nearly every night, watching and tracking the heavens, then recording their observations. But in all the nights in all the years this magus had studied the heavens, he'd never seen anything like the sequence of phenomena he'd watched unfold over the previous nine months.

The magi—plural of magus—studied the skies out of religious conviction. They had done this for more than a thousand years. Many ancient people assigned significance to planetary movement, but the magi were masters. Many historians believe that their forbears developed the very original theories for predicting people's destinies by matching the alignments of heavenly bodies with the seasons of their birth.

Magi believed that human souls have a star counterpart. Half the soul lives in the body and half in a point of light somewhere across the canopy of heaven. At death, the human-bound segment of the soul returns to the star and, depending on virtue or lack thereof, either on to eternal fulfillment or back to rebirth in another human body. In other words, the magi evidently believed in a form of reincarnation based on something similar to what people in India call Karma.

The word *Karma* comes from Sanskrit, though the idea it depicts evolved in several cultures at about the same time in history. It means "action and the action-influence" and describes the self-operating law of cause and effect behind everything.

This worldview is sometimes called *monism*. Monism sees the universe as *one*. It is sovereign and eternal, and nothing else beyond exists. Given enough time, everything in this one universe returns to balanced equilibrium. Nothing new comes in; nothing old goes out. One side of the equation must balance the other. This is Karma; Karma is cosmic algebra—which, perhaps not incidentally, was probably invented by ancient magi.

One of the most poetic descriptions of this idea comes from our own American essayist Ralph Waldo Emerson in his masterpiece "Compensation."

> Thus is the universe alive. All things are moral. That soul, which within us is a sentiment, outside of us is a law. We feel its inspiration; out there in history we can see its fatal strength. "It is in the world, and the world was made by it." Justice is not postponed. A perfect equity adjusts its balance in all parts of life. *Oi chusoi Dios aei enpiptousi*— The dice of God are always loaded. The world looks like a multiplication-table, or a mathematical equation, which, turn it how you will, balances itself. Take what figure you will, its exact value, no more nor less, still returns to you. Every secret is told, every crime is punished, every virtue rewarded, every wrong redressed, in silence and certainty. What we call retribution is the universal necessity by which the whole appears wherever a part appears. If you see smoke, there must be fire. If you see a hand or a limb, you know that the trunk to which it belongs is there behind.

In personal matters, Karma describes the accumulation of all the effects of all the actions of my body, mind, and intuition. As ocean waves rolling toward the shore build up sandbars beneath the surface, so my actions and their results accumulate and steadily build up tendencies that determine the course of our future. Karma makes me responsible for all these deeds, and the universe enforces this responsibility one way or the other.

As Emerson describes the idea, Karma controls more than an individual's destiny. It encompasses the action-energy of *everything* that has ever occurred, past or present, connecting every event back to the influences causing that event and forward to all results initiated by it. Karma goes further still by assigning responsibility and triggering recip-rocation to all participants invested in the action. What-ever goes out bounces back like a boomerang to its source, and when it arrives home it demands compensation. The universe is a giant echo chamber. The piper must be paid. Chickens always come home to roost.

Students of Indian spirituality call the epic Hindu devo-tional work in poetic form *Bhagavad Gita* (the Song of God) the essence of Hindu spirituality. Set as a dramatic dia-logue between a warrior named Arjuna and his charioteer, Krishna—one of the incarnations of God—*Bhagavad Gita* offers one of the first comprehensive treatments of the doc-trine of Karma in recorded history. Modern scholars date it around 500 BCE.

The story begins on a battlefield and then moves to the inner thoughts and motives of the main characters. As Arjuna prepares for battle, he discovers that his enemies are members of his own family and he refuses to fight. Krishna chides Arjuna, reminding him that his position as a soldier obligates him to do battle. Duty must trump sentiment. Every station of life, Krishna claims, prescribes a particular duty. Arjuna's warrior-role has been determined by his past actions and cannot be shunned. Moral living means fulfill-ing duty.

In the *Bhagavad Gita,* Karma stands as a self-perpetuating law of cause and effect, the force that explains and determines all events in the universe. This Hindu tradition identifies Karma in three forms:

- *Sanchita* is negative Karma carried over from previous lives. Knowledge can destroy Sanchita.
- *Prarabhda* are fruits from our lives that can't be removed and must be either enjoyed (if they are good) or endured (if they are bad).
- *Kriyamana* are deeds we're doing in the moment. They can be shed by offering them to God, or mitigated by a teacher acting as an agent of God.

According to the *Bhagavad Gita,* the gods can and do intervene in human affairs. But they are not the final word in creating destiny. Even Krishna must submit to the rule of Sanchita, Prarabhda, and Kriyamana. Like every being, he plays a role bound by duty for which he has been cast as a result of his previous choices. Gods are not sovereign or even eternal. Only Karma has the first and last word.

As Hinduism found its poetic voice in the *Bhagavad Gita,* another spiritual vision emerged from the Ganges Valley of northern India. Every year, like clockwork, monsoon floods returned to the Ganges basin. Destruction, famine, cholera, battles with venomous snakes, and wars between clans competing for scarce resources always followed. In villages like Kapilavastu, Hindu priests chanted their magic Vedas and coaxed their citizens to sacrifice to the gods in the hope of stemming the misery. Yet year upon year the suffering continued.

Around 490 BCE, a savior appeared in Kapilavastu: the child Gautama. Leaders hailed him a miraculous incarnation of the gods. But as a young man, Gautama openly rejected Hindu polytheism. Instead of begging gods to rescue them, Gautama—the Buddha—improvised a new strategy. He sought to defeat suffering through resignation and detachment. He passed on his wisdom as Buddhism's "Four Noble Truths":

- All existence involves suffering.
- All suffering stems from indulging desire.
- All suffering will cease with the suppression of desire.
- To achieve the end of desire a person must follow the "Noble Eightfold Path" of right belief, right aspiration, right speech, right action, right livelihood, right endeavor, right thought, and right meditation.

According to the Buddha, freedom comes only when we acquiesce to suffering and reject our instinctive desires that give suffering power. This Noble Eightfold Path may take many cycles of incarnation to perfect. Life cannot resolve until all Karma—the residue of individual existence—is stripped away. The problem, he noted, is that mere living generates Karma, and Karma itself makes waves in the world that create as well as endure suffering. So as long as we exist, said Buddha, we act. As long as we act, we generate Karma. As long as we make Karma, we must return to atone for what we leave behind. His final solution: Find a way to cease to exist and to be reabsorbed into the motionless underpinning of the universe.

While Indian spiritual leaders defined the karmic theme in their context, virtually the same picture of balance and justice established another civilization thousands of miles to the west in the islands of Greece.

Greek mythology, the original vehicle for what we now call Greek ideals, assigned Ananke the goddess of necessity and gave her the mission to allot to every god and mortal favor or judgment according to their deeds. Nemesis had a complementary role of enforcing right balance and maintaining equilibrium in happiness and fortune. Whenever a god or mortal received more than their fair share, Nemesis evened the score. This belief in a fair and balanced universe personified by the roles and duties of these gods paved the way for the development of a doctrine of reincarnation that eventually emerged in the Orphic and Pythagorean traditions.

Then around 500 BCE, the Greeks' mythical and mystical speculations gelled into a grand unified theory of philosophy. In his *The Republic*, Plato, the great visionary of idealism, defines justice as an individual fulfilling the duty and role assigned him by destiny. With this pronouncement, Plato strikes a chord remarkably similar to the Krishna's lecture to Arjuna in *Bhagavad Gita*.

Plato's *Phaedrus* goes further by defining the nature of soul and its relationship to the material world. Humans, speculates Plato, are souls who have "fallen" into a world of contaminated matter. Those souls who have not tumbled into this tangible existence of time and space remain "gods" living out their roles and duties in a spiritual dimension. Human purpose is to struggle and reclaim our spiritual identity. Plato predicts that this process could take as many as ten reincarnations, interspersed by cycles of one thousand years of reward and punishment assigned according to one's virtue in his or her last incarnation.

Historians scratch their collective bald spots over this puzzling coincidence: One single "theory of everything," recognized by the Hindu word *Karma,* grew to maturity almost simultaneously in two distinct and advanced civilizations—Greece and India—separated by three thousand miles of deserts and mountains.

The parallels are unmistakable: Hinduism, Buddhism, and Greek philosophy all build their systems on an assumption of universal compensation.

- Greeks, Hindus, and some Buddhists believe that gods interact with mortals, but destiny rules all. The cosmos is a closed system of causes and effects. No miracles exist. Karma is not administered by an individual, either divine or mortal. It is an automated system of balance embedded in the DNA of everything.
- The Greek and Indian traditions each see history as a circle repeating itself. We eventually receive back what we give. Every good is a return for prior virtue; every misery is compensation for prior wickedness. They believe even a child tortured in the Holocaust bore responsibility for "attracting" the assault as payback for some prior crime.
- Both civilizations rely on reincarnation to resolve the riddle of justice. A single lifetime can never fully explain why bad things happen to good people and why good things happen to bad people. Prior and future lives have to be added to the equation.
- Some Greeks and Hindus see reincarnation as the return of individual souls who can, through discipline, remember their former lives. Other Greeks and most Buddhists believe that life-forces recycle but individual personalities do not.

Andrew thought a moment, then added, "Karma's also in the Bible."

I wrinkled my face and ran a quick inventory of possible Karma parallels in the Jewish and Christian traditions. Similarities existed, for certain.

- In Paul's first-century letter to a group of churches in Galatia (today known as Turkey) we find: "Don't be misled—you cannot mock the justice of God. You will always harvest what you plant."
- And Jesus' words in Mark's gospel: " 'Consider carefully what you hear,' he continued. 'With the measure you use, it will be measured to you—and even more. Whoever has will be given more; whoever does not have, even what he has will be taken from him.' "
- In Jesus' great Sermon on the Mount, we read: "Do not judge others, and you will not be judged. For you will be treated as you treat others. The standard you use in judging is the standard by which you will be judged."
- Explaining that Israel's suffering comes upon them because of their past disregard for established standards of right and wrong, one of the Jewish prophets writes: "They have planted the wind and will harvest the whirlwind."
- The epic poem "Job" debates the hard and fast rule of retribution. One of Job's accusers articulates a belief commonly accepted at the time, though denounced by Job and later by God: "My experience shows that those who plant trouble and cultivate evil will harvest the same."
- Moses laid down the primary description for reciprocal justice: "But if there is further injury, the

punishment must match the injury: a life for a life, an eye for an eye, a tooth for a tooth, a hand for a hand, a foot for a foot, a burn for a burn, a wound for a wound, a bruise for a bruise."

- Moses added that a failure to abide by the standards God articulates guarantees dire consequences: "But if you fail to keep your word, then you will have sinned against the Lord, and you may be sure that your sin will find you out."

"I guess you're partly right," I concurred.

Andrew nodded in respect for the concession. "I like Proverbs," he said. "Simple common sense, usable stuff for Tuesday. All about actions and consequences."

"Solomon wrote Proverbs," I said, wondering how much more I should add. "I suppose Solomon is as good a biblical example of Karma—good and bad—as anyone."

I knew more of Solomon's story than I took the time to unload to Andrew. People call Solomon wise, maybe the wisest man ever. But while he started strong, he ended his life a pitiful wreck.

Three thousand years ago this Hebrew king mastered all the scientific knowledge available to him. He built an empire with magnetic charisma, and his business sense brought him massive wealth and international respect. He managed people with savvy and prudent practicality. Solomon seemed to grasp the details and moral lessons of history like few have ever done. He then used what he envisioned to shrewdly anticipate the future.

Solomon understood that virtue brings a rich life. In his collection of wise sayings titled *Proverbs* in the Jewish and Christian Bibles, he wrote the following:

No harm comes to the godly,
  but the wicked have their fill of trouble.

Trouble chases sinners,
  while blessings reward the righteous.

There is treasure in the house of the godly,
  but the earnings of the wicked bring trouble.

Karma?

Yet for all his success and touted wisdom, by the end of his life Solomon came to consider all he had gained a colossal waste. "Vanity," he called it at a time when a moral cancer had eaten away the core of his soul. Solomon understood, taught, and wrote that choices bring consequences. Yet he couldn't practice what he preached and paid the price.

Never able to bridle his sexual appetite, Solomon consummated some seven hundred "diplomatic" marriages arranged with daughters of foreign leaders with whom he sought favor. These marriages introduced almost unfathomable relational complexity and confusion into his life. They seem to have twisted, even poisoned his heart. In time, Solomon reaped the seeds he'd recklessly sown, and the harvest doomed him. He died bitter, broken, and depressed.

Two collections of Solomon's wise sayings, Proverbs and Ecclesiastes, sit at the literal center of the Christian Bible. The former offers promises that those who do good find rewards in return. The latter is a confessional of the ruthless judgment leveled against those who defy the final rule of justice.

Andrew jolted me out of my reflections. "So I can add the Bible alongside the other holy books built on Karma. Right?"

"Understand that the Bible answers the challenges Karma raises in a very distinct way," I answered. "It makes justice personal, championed and delivered by a Person, something other and beyond the mechanical laws of the universe."

This distinction suddenly grew quite clear to me. At first glance, the Judeo-Christian commitment of retributive justice seems parallel to the core teachings of Karma. Good comes from good, bad from bad. That much is consistent. But underlying the concept of justice in the Bible rests an assumption that God made the world according to a natural law that rewards fairness and punishes injustice. The biblical tradition of judgment and blessing flows ultimately from the hand of a personal, sovereign God and not merely a predictable cosmos. Behind everything stands a Person, not clockwork. Here I'd struck one of the chief distinctions in the way Andrew and I looked at the world. Justice returns all things. On that we could agree. But is justice personal or impersonal? That's the question!

Ancestors of the magus astronomer who stood on the tower that night had come to live in Babylon five hundred years earlier. Since their arrival, the magi had held almost continual positions of significant influence as soothsayers and magicians in the courts of kings. They had come originally from Media, the old kingdom of Northern Persia—today's Iran—where they had served as priests in the dominant Persian religion that dated back at least a thousand years.

Their high regard in Persia had ended in 521 BCE, when Darius I took the throne. Darius favored the teachings of the Zoroastrians, who rejected monism and saw the world as a cosmic battleground between competing and equal spiritual forces: one good, one evil. Darius had little affection for the old religion and wanted the magi out of power and out of Persia. Sixteen years into his rule, in 505 BCE, Darius I turned his preference into policy. He decreed a new Iranian calendar that replaced traditional feasts with rites honoring the Zoroastrian faith. Facing forced compliance or expulsion, or worse, many magi fled Persia.

Some—the ancestors of our particular stargazer—journeyed west into Babylon. Others turned east toward India. A few adventurers ventured west as far as the Greek islands, perhaps paving the way for Persia's ambitious armies, which would follow that path just a few years later, igniting the infamous Greek and Persian wars.

It was at the time of this magian exile that artists and thinkers in both Greece and India began to articulate the idea we now recognize as Karma. Coincidence?

To be fair, the seeds of this idea existed in both Greece and India prior to the magi's arrival. But it isn't until after 500 BCE that the puzzle pieces converge into unified worldviews that find expression in the great works of philosophy and art produced in both of these cultures.

Did the magi play a part in molding the fragments of an intuition into one coherent doctrine? Did this provocative new minority influence their hosts the way a small but potent herb flavors a pot of soup? Were the magi the Johnny Appleseeds of Karma? Was Karma the first gift of the magi?

On that particular evening five centuries after his fathers had settled in Babylon, this magus and his apprentice stood on a rooftop studying the stars with one specific purpose: He needed one final reading to confirm his thesis. If his calculations held, the next day he would finally convene a meeting of the council and make his unprecedented recommendation. If he was right, their destiny, and the destiny of the entire world, might hang in the balance.

In the introduction to the Jutaka, one of the foundational Buddhist texts written down sometime around the third century BCE, Sumedha, purportedly an earlier incarnation of the Buddha, acknowledges the trap that Karma levels against humanity. He longs for a way to accelerate through the cycles of reincarnation and hasten to his freedom. Karma, for him, is doom.

> There is, there must be, an escape
> Impossible there should not be!
> I'll make the search and find the way
> Which from existence shall release.

Is there a way out of the clutch of Karma?

If the magi did indeed sow seeds of this theory wherever they moved, could they also have become aware of the doom their philosophy leveled? Could they have begun looking for a way out themselves?

In September, 3 BCE, this magus studying the skies in Babylon noticed the first of a series of phenomena that he and others took as a significant sign.

His curiosity was piqued when he and his student watched Jupiter, the largest planet in the solar system, known as the King Planet in most cultures, move into conjunction with the star Regulus, called Rex, or King, by the

Romans and Sharu, or King, by the Babylonians. The King Planet and the King Star set in the constellation Leo, or Lion, aligned in the month that a minority group in Babylon, the Jews, celebrated their new year. He was fascinated and kept watching.

Over the following weeks and months, the magus observed Jupiter circle back across the field of fixed stars for a second, then for a third rendezvous with Regulus. These circles traced by Jupiter's wandering across Leo looked like halos or crowns over the fixed star. What could it mean? The coronation of a new king? Who? Where? As a learned man, this magus knew the Jewish prophecies of a coming great king from the clan of Judah, the Lion, who would usher in a new era of peace. Could this birth be the sign of that Great King?

The riddle became clearer nine months later. After its three conjunctions with Regulus, Jupiter moved toward another, more brilliant meeting that climaxed in June 2 BCE: Jupiter conjoined Venus.

The marvel would have been the talk of Babylon—a spectacular sight, unlike anything anyone alive at the time had ever seen: two prominent planets side by side, each lending their full brilliance in a light that appeared to the naked eye as one luminous star. As the magus stood on his tower that night—watching the paired planets rise from the western horizon—he realized something else: He was facing Jerusalem.

The pieces fit. His scholar's head and mystic's heart conjoined as one bright and bold conviction. Tomorrow he would call the council. He would lay out his evidence, explain his conclusions, answer questions and rebuttals, then propose a plan of action—a diplomatic journey toward

Jerusalem in Israel to honor and pay tribute to this new king who perhaps offered a way—*the* way—out of the eternal crippling doom of Karma that he and every magus with him felt so completely.

3

GUILT BY ASSOCIATION

Those who know him call him *Walker,* because that's what he does—sometimes twenty miles a day. His given name is Steven, and I'm likely to run into him every few weeks in any one of the coffee shops I frequent. Anyone who meets Walker never forgets the encounter. Last week I saw him strolling along the side of the road, his walking stick swinging in his hand, with two truant teenage boys trying to keep pace. He had engaged them in some topic that obviously fascinated them. What else could get two teen boys to walk that fast?

Walker is a taut, fire-eyed sixty-year-old Navy SEAL with a grizzled ponytail hanging down the middle of his back. Picture that. Any given conversation with him could alternate between a Stephen King horror tale, his own Vietnam horror story, chaos theory, his spite against organized Christianity, and the steamy romance novel he's reading at the time. On this particular morning, Walker burst through the doors of the Caribou Coffee shop, ordered something, then turned and recognized me. Immediately he came over and sat down to begin his usual interrogation.

"What are you writing?"

"I'm working on my next book."

"Oh, Karma," he shot back as he recalled our last happenstance dialogue. "Not done yet?" Walker held out his palms as if to say, *You idiot! It's only forty-five thousand words!*

"It's coming," I said with more deliberate coolness than I felt, and nodding to signal, *Hey, got it all under control.*

"You know, of all the stuff you religious clowns spew, this twist on Karma comes closest to making sense . . . close," he added shortly. "Me, I believe in survival. That's it: how to just breathe and fight and keep my genes in the pool. Breeding is life. What are you writing now?"

I looked down at the computer screen to call up my mental RAM. "Ah, how bad directions blew up the world," I answered cryptically.

Walker raised his eyebrows and grunted for me to explain.

I cleared my throat, then read aloud the outcome of my morning's labor:

June 28, 1914: A chauffeur drove through Sarajevo with Archduke Ferdinand, the heir apparent of the Austro-Hungarian Empire. Because of attempts on the archduke's life, travel plans changed at the last minute. The details of the change of plans, however, did not get to the driver, who inadvertently steered down the wrong street and into a mob protesting the archduke's presence. Gavrilo Princip, a conspirator plotting Ferdinand's assassination, happened to be standing on the very street corner where the chauffeur stopped to correct his mistake. Princip seized the moment, pulled his gun and fired, killing both Ferdinand and his wife, Sophia. Turmoil erupted, and in time, because of a tangled thread of international alliances and treaties, the world fell into a great firestorm known now as World War I. From that grew the Russian Revolution, the Great Depression, then World War II, the Chinese Revolution, the Cold War, and the rise of Islamic terrorism. All hell broke loose from one wrong turn, and according to the law of Karma, this one ill-informed driver is partly responsible.

"No fire," said Walker, shaking his head with a disdain I didn't understand. "You have to learn to write words with fire, not syllables."

"Well how would you tell the story?" I answered defensively.

"The Serbs always fight for survival. The religious insanity they posture is only an excuse. The only fights that matter explode over who controls the land. Religion is a meaningless cancer on our species, a petty distraction to justify the real issue: controlling the land. . . . But we've been over that question, you and me, and we agree to disagree, and we are still friends, yes?" Walker smirked and grabbed my forearm like a vise grip.

"Of course," I said. "You're Serbian, aren't you?" I added, remembering that he'd mentioned this during more than one of our previous conversations.

"Indeed," Walker replied, thrusting out his chest. Then he added, almost in passing, "Princip was my cousin."

I chuckled. "Your cousin? Gavrilo Princip was your cousin?"

"What? Am I lying?" Walker's nostrils flared and the arteries in his neck swelled. "Three generations back, yes. He's flesh and bone, and I'm shameless-proud of it."

My head spun, and it wasn't the caffeine. Walker had a brilliant mind; I knew that. But his stories sometimes teetered near the edge of freakish. This seemed too bizarre to accept without a fight. "Gavrilo Princip was your cousin," I said again incredulously, with a tone I meant as a dare, to say, *Prove it!*

Walker shrugged, as if to say in return, *Fine, don't believe me. . . .*

How weird can the world be? I'm sitting in a franchise coffee shop reading an online *Encyclopedia Americana* article about the accidental trigger of World War I, trying to write a "fiery" introduction to a chapter about unintended consequences in a book about a conversation I had with a young man curious about Karma and the meaning of Jesus' life, and in walks the assassin Gavrilo Princip's cousin, who sits down beside me with an iced mocha latte and begins rattling on about social Darwinism. And people say everything happens by chance! I say things happen for a reason!

"So, 'your cousin' started World War I," I said, still staring suspiciously at his tan, leathered features.

"Oh no," Walker smirked. He stood and tapped me on the shoulder with his walking stick. "Oh no, the chauffeur did that!" He winked, took three long strides toward the door, and was gone.

I stared at Walker as he crossed the street between lines of traffic and passed out of sight. *Small things make up the world*, I thought. Gazing through the shop's tinted window reminded me of a radio piece I'd recently heard on NPR. The feature reporter explained a sociological theory known as "broken windows." The idea claims that low-level crimes such as littering and vandalism create an environment that breeds worse crimes. According to this theory, law enforcement can reduce overall crime by simply clamping down on seemingly insignificant mayhem like graffiti. Little things make the world.

Some Dutch researchers conducted a series of clever experiments to test this idea, specifically whether small amounts of environmental disorder would induce people to steal. The researchers left an envelope containing a five-euro note (worth about $6.26) hanging conspicuously from a mailbox. When the ground around the mailbox was clear of trash, 13 percent of passersby stole the envelope. But when the mailbox was surrounded by trash, 25 percent took the money. When they added graffiti on the mailbox, 27 percent stole it.

The point: Petty things have consequences, often far more complicated and destructive than we would logically expect. And since the universe never forgets, we're held responsible for even the small things we do and for the rippling bigger things our 'doing' ultimately triggers. If you're an egg-headed chauffeur, here's the bleak news: Your "little" accident "caused" the first great war—and from there all the bloody horrors that marred the twentieth century.

"So you admit there's Karma in the Bible," Andrew pressed.

I'd already conceded this, so I veered back to retrace my first objection to Andrew's metaphysical optimism. "Like I said, Andrew, a good life is hard to hold together. You buy the Karma deal, you get the whole package."

"Look, I've spent most of my life playing victim. My dad treated me like toxic waste. I blamed him for everything wrong in my life because it gave me an excuse not to take responsibility. That's over. I decide. My response to other people's stupidity, not their stupidity itself, decides my destiny. I'm in control of what happens, good or bad. I own it. I don't blame anyone anymore."

"Commendable, I guess," I said. "Karma holds you responsible all right."

"That's reality."

"What about good intentions that result in not-so-good outcomes?" I asked. "Are we judged by motives or real results?"

"I don't know what you mean." Andrew shifted in his chair and folded his arms.

"Here's one example that's fresh for me. You know ABC's reality show *Extreme Makeover: Home Edition?*"

"Yeah," Andrew answered. I tried to picture him watching this show—a troupe of kindhearted Home Depot types bussing around the country restoring homes of hard-on-their-luck families. He didn't seem the maudlin type, and I suspected he'd seldom watched.

"Well, in an episode my kids watched last week, the remodelers took on a project for a young family in New York. Joe had three small boys and he'd recently lost his wife to leukemia—I think her name was Anne-Marie. . . ." I relayed to him a snapshot version of the episode:

Before Anne-Marie's sickness, she and Joe had planned to renovate their small house to accommodate their growing family. But medical bills ate away Joe's savings and the project stalled. That's when the *Extreme Makeover* design team came to the rescue. After sending Joe and his boys away for a short vacation, they went to work and in a matter of one week rebuilt the small two-bedroom abode into a completely new home. The result seemed perfect for Joe and his boys.

But one problem remained. The house, rebuilt in memory of Anne-Marie, took the form of a shrine. Her pictures hung on the wall. A special "secret lounge" was tucked in behind Joe's bedroom. In every room a ghost of Anne-Marie hung in the air. It was a nice deed, but the house now binds this poor family to her death. The project felt good and generous. But what happens when another woman wants to come into their lives, someone willing to be a wife and mother to them? She'd have to live in Anne-Marie's mausoleum and never escape the shadow. And how could Joe ever sell the house and start a new life? The whole thing is a feel-good version of bondage.

"So generosity can backfire. Big deal," Andrew said.

"It *is* a big deal. We're never smart enough to predict outcomes, even when we intend good. And Karma doesn't obey motives. And it doesn't discriminate. It's not personal; it's cold, calculating mechanics, with no capacity to make an exception. Karma answers with hard-core reality in response to what *actually* happens. They never wanted it so, but Ty Pennington and his crew screwed up this family's future, and Karma makes them culpable."

Maybe age and experience has made me a skeptic. I do grieve the loss of idealistic innocence, but here in conversation with Andrew, realism gave me boldness. Had I hit a fundamental vulnerability in Karma's prescription?

According to Isaac Newton, the world functions like a simple game of billiards, with one ball striking another, and then another, and so forth. But when we imagine doubling or tripling the number of billiard balls on the table, then shoving them all at once against one another, then simultaneously rocking the table, then adding in three or four lopsided balls . . . Well, causes and effects still happen, but very quickly everything becomes too enmeshed and random to distinguish. How could anyone with a human-sized brain track, let alone manage, Karma in a world far more complex than any pool table?

A flurry of examples akin to *Extreme Makeover* complexity paraded through my mind: *It's a Wonderful Life*, Ellen, Orson Welles, Yellowstone, *Chaos*, Ravi. They were too many and too detailed to dump on Andrew, though they appeared to me an overwhelming tide of support for my skepticism.

It's a Wonderful Life. Frank Capra's warm and fuzzy post–World War II holiday film makes a case for the power of unintended consequences, albeit from the positive side of the ledger. The story suggests that one man's life can positively affect the world even when he's not aware that any good is happening.

George Bailey, Capra's hero, dutifully defers his own ambition to ensure the well-being of those around him. Near the climax, however, George discovers the pitiable truth that selflessness leaves *him* holding the bill run up by someone else's incompetency, a bill he has to pay but can't.

Salvation arrives when Clarence the angel drops in to show George how the world would have been had he never been born. "You've been given a great gift, George," explains Clarence, "a chance to see what the world would be like without you."

In a surreal vision of nonexistence, George and Clarence encounter Mr. Gower, a hapless drunk. Gower, a former pharmacist, poisoned a child because George (his employee in the actual world) had not been there to correct the mistake. They walk through Bedford Falls, now named Pottersville, a cesspool of corruption because George had not been around to foil Old Man Potter, the town villain. George learns that thousands of sailors died on a ship in the Pacific War because Harry Bailey, George's brother, was not there to save them—because George hadn't been there to save Harry, who fell through a frozen pond and drowned at the age of nine.

Capra believes we all leave our mark on the world, in the infinitely intricate calculus of interrelationships. But in his optimistic vision, George's actions and their results— and by extension, those of all good men—would be *all* and *only* good.

Wishful thinking on Capra's part, scoffs the realist. An equally dark side haunts this same paradigm. Even the best "George" in the world has made his share of mistakes and accidental wrong turns down dead-end streets. And if we follow the story's logic, every one of those choices would also spur consequences we can't imagine or predict or control.

Yes, George Bailey's courage played a part in saving a transport full of sailors. But what if by deciding to take over his father's failing building-and-loan, and therefore not travel to Europe as he planned, George Bailey missed a chance to make some other small choice, maybe something that would have eventually led to uncovering evidence of Germany's pending invasion of Poland, which, had it happened, could have stopped the war altogether? Who is to say what might have been had George made other decisions? In the least, the choices he did make would have cast as many shadows as they did beams of light.

Had Capra been born with a more cynical temperament, he might have cast *It's a Wonderful Life* as a negative film, made it a dark comedy and the title satirical, a world where all of Bailey's nobly intended actions turned upside-down and ugly.

Of course, we want to believe that all our best intentions have only the best results, that the law of Karma and the sum of its parts adds up to a total that is simple and easy to calculate and always plainly fair. Skeptics and others who have been around the block a few times realize things are never that simple.

Ellen. A friend I had known for years had been living this lesson in a deeply personal way. Ellen works as a manager in a large not-for-profit organization, and at the time faced one of her deepest leadership crises. Two of her employees had a very emotional disagreement over the strategy to pursue in a project that involved both of their departments. Ellen pulled these parties together and attempted to guide them toward consensus.

Ellen's experiment in civility blew up in her face. The meeting turned into a volcano of personal accusations. When Ellen stepped in to mediate the argument, this peacemaking also backfired. The warring parties each thought Ellen had sided with the other, and both turned their fury on her, accusing her of mismanagement and ignoring corporate dysfunction.

In retrospect, perhaps Ellen should have made a unilateral decision in the controversy, forgoing any attempt at consensus. Her goodwill gestures from the best motives added fuel to the fires of conflict.

After Ellen's repeated attempts to bring a peaceful resolution, one of her employees resigned. The other asked to be transferred to work under a different supervisor. In the real world of Karma dynamics, $1 + 1 \neq 2$. What should be, almost never is.

Orson Welles. The famous actor and director's voice echoed into my mental picture. As a creative genius, Welles blazed amazing trails in American storytelling—on stage, in film, and on radio. But for all his groundbreaking accomplishments, Welles is perhaps most known for a prank that inadvertently turned into a national fiasco—his *War of the Worlds* radio broadcast.

On October 30, 1938, Welles aired live a Halloween episode of the American radio drama series *Mercury Theatre on the Air,* broadcast over the CBS network. Welles hoped to entertain as well as dramatically spook his listeners. What he actually accomplished turned into imagination-terrorism.

Welles staged an adaptation of H. G. Wells' novel *The War of the Worlds,* where humans attempt to fend off a Martian invasion of Earth. What made the show so devastatingly frightening was its staged authenticity. The first forty minutes of the hour-long program were presented as a series of simulated news bulletins, suggesting to listeners that an actual Martian invasion was under way.

People across America panicked. Thousands called the police. Many in New England fled their homes. People flocked to churches to pray. They improvised gas masks. And worse: Miscarriages and premature births were reported. In general, people went hysterical. The end—they believed—had come!

Welles understood he was playing with mass emotion, but he never intended hysteria. Hysteria happened. Does he now bear some cosmic responsibility for the firestorm his story around the campfire actually sparked? If Earl and Buddha and Newton and Andrew are right, the universe keeps score, and yes, Welles is culpable.

Yellowstone. What an amazing piece of the planet! A few summers back, my two boys and I explored its back trails on our annual guys' adventure.

During a hike we came upon a lone national park ranger peering through a pair of binoculars and making notes in a journal. He greeted us, and seeing an opportunity to "inform the public," began to explain his assignment.

"Yellowstone has taught us the limitations of human intervention," he began. "Our do-good efforts nearly decimated, in fifty years, a balance nature had wrought over many millennia."

"What are you looking at?" Matthew, who was ten at the time, asked him.

He handed Matthew his binoculars. "Look down there." He pointed down the valley. "Do you see that beaver dam?" The ranger helped Matthew aim his view.

His six-year-old brother, Michael, pressed in and reached up for his turn.

"That beaver dam is a good sign. Yellowstone is recovering. Beaver help."

The ranger then gave us a crash course in Yellowstone's recent ecological history. In 1872, President Grant set aside these two million spectacular acres, larger than Delaware and Rhode Island combined, as our first national park. But shortly afterward, the newly formed National Park Service began to tinker with their new wonderland.

"Rangers started killing wolves to protect elk, which they falsely believed were headed for extinction. The elk herd grew and started crowding out antelope and deer." The boys' attention drifted and they started squabbling over the binoculars. The ranger turned his focus to me.

"To protect the antelope and deer, rangers killed off all the predators. By 1930, most of the wolves, cougars, and coyotes were gone. Meanwhile, the exploding elk herd devoured all the young aspen and willow trees. With no young aspens, the beavers began to disappear. And with no beavers, the meadows dried up, and more animals vanished. Except the bears: Without wolves and cougars to keep them in check, the bear population more than doubled, and that brought a whole new round of problems."

I began to get the picture. "What about the big fire?" I asked. The valley below us still bore scars that even I, a city guy, could easily identify.

"That's another thing!" he added. "In the 1940s we started putting out every forest fire. Remember Smokey the Bear? Well, with forty years of tinder building on the forest floor when the big blaze hit in '88, it exploded into an inferno and torched a third of the park."

"So why the turnaround now?" I asked, reaching for the binoculars myself and aiming them down toward the beaver dam.

"Wolves," he said. "We finally realized that playing God didn't work. Good intentions, disastrous results. We brought the wolves back, and now slowly everything is returning to the right balance. It's just naïve to think we can ever manage the intricate balance of nature."

Chaos. I recalled James Gleick's watershed book that christens this complexity with the name *chaos* and gives it its own category in science. Gleick gathers an assortment of scientific observations, theories, and experiments for his orderly assessment of the disorders of the universe. Why does weather behave so randomly? Why do traffic snares appear and then disappear with no evident cause? How can one seemingly minuscule fragment of insecticide compound through an environmental system until it nearly wipes out the bald eagle population in North America? Gleick concludes that the only reasonable answer to the riddle of chaos is that everything in the universe is minutely connected in a relationship of fine-line causes and effects so intertwined that to know them all would be to know everything there is to know.

At one time, Gleick reflects, knowing everything actually seemed possible. Back in the seventeenth century, Isaac Newton and those who followed him in what was called the Enlightenment elevated science as the highest arbiter of truth. And once Newton's theories took root in Western culture, people came to trust that science could and would eventually isolate, observe, and explain every sequence in nature. We really might come to know everything. It could take centuries, but science had the tools. All causes lead to observable effects, and all effects trace back to recognizable causes, all following a tight and consistent set of natural laws.

Then came Einstein, and after him the quirky discoveries of quantum physics. Suddenly certainty fell to dust and ashes. Scattering particles spewed from an exploding star in a distant galaxy a hundred million years ago even now settle on the pool table in a Newark tavern and turn the eight ball ever so slightly as it rolls toward the side left pocket. A very near-miss can be partly blamed on one too many beers, but also on the stardust and a million other tiny variations that comprise that particular pool table.

Everything in the physical world connects with everything else. As Edward Lorenz's first computer-generated weather model demonstrated, a butterfly flapping its wings in the jungles of Nigeria can trigger a hurricane off the coast of Florida. There are no singular causes and singular effects, and whatever order is observed by us is really nothing more than the mathematical probability in the monstrous bell curve of our total human experience.

Newton said, "For every action there is an equal and opposite reaction." Now we know that "for every action there are an infinite and unpredictable series of reactions." The chain of actions and results grows long and intertwined, much too long to trace and manage. Newton's billiard world has now dissolved into the denser, relative world of postmodern uncertainty.

Western pop culture tries to democratize Karma into a simple pool table vision of reality. But the ancient minds who gave original voice to the Karma concept thousands

of years ago understood intuitively what Gleick and Lorenz
and others have now demonstrated scientifically: Things
are very, very, very complicated, because everything ties
together. Small and seemingly discrete actions can—and
will—kick out unpredictable outcomes. Forests do not exist,
only trees. As the old proverb cleverly puts it:

> For lack of a nail, the shoe was lost;
> For lack of a shoe, the horse was lost;
> For lack of a horse, the rider was lost;
> For lack of a rider, the battle was lost;
> For lack of a battle, the kingdom was lost!

Ravi Zacharias. His book *The Lotus and the Cross* tackles
the myth of personal Karma by imagining an "interfaith
dialogue" between Jesus and Buddha. The topic of their
discussion is the suffering of a young woman named Priya,
who before her death was forced into prostitution. After
the Buddha explains that she has attracted the suffering
because of Karma from her former life, Priya responds:

> This is perplexing. It is at once my greatest hope and my
> greatest puzzle. My friends and I have often talked about
> this. Whose Karma is being worked out when each life
> is wrapped around so many? I wonder: Are my parents
> also paying for past lives through my tragedy? Are my
> customers paying when I sell my diseased body to them?
> What about the baby that I gave up? Was that its Karma,
> even before it knew anything about good or bad? I mean,
> trying to reach for an answer in this karmic cycle is like
> putting your hand in a bucket of glue and then trying to
> wipe it clean. Everything you touch becomes sticky and
> there's nowhere to wash it off.

As I relay Ravi's brilliant passage, I wonder if this Eastern understanding that all things are connected somehow explains why the cultures of the Orient, which gave birth to the doctrine of Karma, remain collective societies. One person's good fortune comes not as a result of his or her immediate preceding good actions, but through some next-to-infinite sequence of events stretching back beyond the distant horizon of history.

As I sat with Andrew, I couldn't help but empathize with his yearning for a simple, single lever that could move every piece of life with one small nudge. Of course, small nudges do make things move, but never in ways we predict. One boulder budges and sets off a rock slide! I couldn't share Andrew's faith that such a simple, single lever can exist. If individual Karma exists at all, it does not exist as Earl and Andrew imagine it. Attempts to manage causes to effects the way Earl attempts his "list" seem like naïve, wishful thinking in the face of a big world that responds to small changes but never in ways we expect.

One last example of this tied my stomach in knots. I pictured again my once vibrant, grinning father, now motionless and helpless on his bed in the ICU. No. Our levers are not strong or specific enough, no matter how carefully we place them or how hard and tenaciously we tug on them.

Andrew took a deep breath. I waited for him to speak. "I still have to take responsibility for myself and my choices. I've learned, finally, that I can't count on anyone else to carry me. Karma might be a cold and calculating way to live, but it's fair."

"Sure, we have to take responsibility for our lives," I said. "But to assume we can fix our lives is a leap of faith that doesn't have any evidence from human experience to support it. It is infinitely simpler to knock down tall buildings with airplanes than it is to construct them. Bad things happen more easily than good things. The street philosopher Murphy said it best: 'If something can go wrong, it will.' "

"So what am I supposed to do, quit trying?" Andrew fired back. "A lot of good *that* did me! That kind of thinking landed me in a Dumpster in an alley, nearly dying of an overdose. This isn't helping!" He stared at me with a flash of frustration and near anger.

"Of course we try to do right. All of us do," I conceded. "But it's mathematically impossible and therefore foolish for me to expect 'good' Karma to ever outpace my 'bad' Karma, even after a thousand lifetimes. Try as I might, for every good effort, three bad results follow. Paul, one of the early Christian teachers, put it this way in a letter he wrote to Jesus-followers in Rome: 'I don't want to do what is wrong, but I do it anyway.' That's me, Andrew. Entropy stacks the odds against me."

"I thought your message was supposed to be good news."

"Not first. First it's bad news," I replied.

"That disillusions me," Andrew said with a deadpan look.

"Me too. But maybe that's okay," I added. "Maybe our illusions *should* be dissed."

SCAMMING THE SYSTEM

"You've never been in treatment," Andrew announced flatly.

"No, not exactly," I admitted.

"Then you can't understand. You've never lain awake in a pool of your own sweat, scheming how to steal Grandma's silver just so you could stick another needle in your arm."

"But I have a drug of choice. I've been addicted to this—" I nodded at the now nearly empty room. "I'm a pastor and the son, grandson, and great-grandson of pastors. Religion is the family business, and I understand the gig. It pays big time; not money, but influence, respect, and fear. People treat me like an authority figure in areas of their lives where they're vulnerable. That gives me power. Power is addicting. Sometimes I'm tempted to do the equivalent of stealing silver just to keep it. My biggest challenge: I work in a church, an environment that feeds my weakness. I'm like a sober alcoholic working as a bartender. Sure, I've never been in your shoes, but you've never been in mine. Don't assume I'm any stronger than you!"

"Fair enough," Andrew said. "So why do you teach religion if it's dangerous—" then he added—"and I think it is, by the way."

I'd asked myself this question a thousand times, and I have as many answers. On that occasion one came to mind in a single memory: a book I'd once read and the name of the author, E. Stanley Jones. *What would E. Stanley Jones say about teaching religion?*

I started shaving at age three. My father had a dark, coarse beard and he loved to use a mug and cake of soap with a brush to lather up. I loved being there with him. I still remember the smell of the horsehair bristles when he'd whip the soap into froth and then smudge some on my cheeks. He'd sometimes remove the blades from one of his safety razors and pull up a stool beside the sink, and together we'd stare into the mirror and scrape our faces clean. My mother has a photograph of this scene hanging on her bathroom wall.

In junior high, this game—barging into my father's world—graduated to money. Every night he'd empty the change from his pockets onto the kitchen counter, and if I got there soon enough—before one of my sisters—it was mine for the taking. When I turned fourteen, he taught me to drive his 1946 Willys Jeep on the dirt roads around our home. At sixteen, I found the keys on a hook beside the front door—passive permission to drive it to school.

Then in my senior year, my father opened another door into his soul: He allowed me to start raiding his library.

The first book I swiped changed my life forever: *Christ at the Round Table* by E. Stanley Jones, an acquaintance of my grandfather and an American expatriate living in India during the 1920s.

In *Christ at the Round Table*, Jones describes a series of forums he initiated in India. He invited leading figures from Hindu, Buddhist, Muslim, and Christian spiritual traditions to compare the outcomes of their personal spiritual journeys. Participants could not debate dogma. They simply answered the question "How is your faith working in your own life?"

The book relays some remarkable stories. According to Jones, most participants shared a common understanding that they needed something beyond themselves—that the course of their lives generated a kind of debris and their religious disciplines gave them strategies to deal with this debris. But few claimed success in their quests. The "stuff" had to go somewhere, yet no one seemed to know where. Dogmas and doctrines aside, religion as a practical matter, says Jones, doesn't really work in its prime objective.

I usually keep a scissors handy when I read the newspaper. I like to clip stories I might later use in my writing and speaking. Lately I've been collecting stories for this book, and a few months back my scissors paid off.

"When we throw something away, what does *away* mean?" asked Ari Derfel. "There's no such thing as 'away.' "

Derfel decided to illustrate his point. For twelve months in 2007, the thirty-five-year-old catering company owner stored all his personal waste inside his Berkeley, California, apartment. Derfel struck upon the idea after looking for statistics about how much refuse each human produces. Unimpressed with the abstract data, he decided to see (and smell) for himself—empirically—by not throwing anything away for one year. The result: ninety-six cubic feet of flattened metal cans, milk jugs, soiled paper towels, stacks of newspapers, etc. His putrid lesson: We humans make a mess.

Moral lesson aside, once Ari Derfel wrapped up his little theatrical experiment, he still faced the perennial question "What do I do with it all now?" "What?" Indeed! It still had to go somewhere.

Each person leaves behind a measurable trash footprint that contributes to the garbage buildup on our planet. More damaging perhaps, we also generate residue when our moral choices run afoul with the irrevocable laws of the universe. We leave spiritual trash footprints. And like used Q-Tips and spent nuclear fuel, our moral garbage can't be ignored. Our Karma, as it is called, has to go somewhere. This is religion's dilemma. What do we do with our stuff?

My friend Mindy and her family and some close friends once rented a houseboat for a weeklong cruise down the northern stretch of the Mississippi River. Five days into the trip, the toilet clogged. As "the crew" worked to plunge out the blockage, pressure built in the tank. You guessed it. The tank sprung a pinhole leak, which sprayed sewer contents at the force of jet propulsion. Stuff blew everywhere. She can hardly get the following story out without busting a rib: "We had it in our hair, on our faces. It got into the light sockets, everywhere! Surprise!" laughs Mindy.

History is littered with the improvised storage depots we humans have attempted to construct in order to dump, ditch, or better yet, destroy bad Karma. We're ingeniously creative with strategies, schemes, and scams that all fall under the widest definition of religion. Three are most common:

1. "Eat, drink, and be merry!"
2. "Presto chango!"
3. "Buck up!"

One strategy we humans follow to cope with bad Karma is to work at ignoring it. Call it the eat-drink-and-be-merry-for-tomorrow-we-die philosophy of life. Faced with the incalculable burden of personal responsibility, Andrew (like so many of us) blew off tomorrow for a series of momentary highs. Ignore the cost! And why not? If we're doomed, why worry? In ancient Hinduism, the god Krishna personified this approach. Krishna infamously thumbs his nose at temperance. His game: Party hardy and live like you can outrun Karma.

Krishna has disciples, like Giacomo Puccini, the great composer of operas. To earn extra money for cigarettes—they were a passion for him—Puccini began to steal pipes from the church organ he played every Sunday and then sell them as scrap metal. To conceal his crime, he contrived to play only notes on the organ that didn't use the missing pipes. His trickery worked for a while. But as he continued pilfering, his musical robbing-(St.) Peter-to-pay-Puccini hustle became more and more difficult to hide. Eventually the holes in his music-making spoke for themselves. Scamming the system goes only so far.

Other examples hit closer to home. I recently met a man who lost his life savings in the Madoff financial scandal. Like so many, he suspected that the investment returns he was getting were just a bit too good to be true. And like so many, he kept investing regardless. Now he's learned the hard way that no one can outpace the laws of mathematics.

The Madoff crime made front pages all over the world. The former chairman of NASDAQ and principal of Bernard L. Madoff Investment Securities corralled top net worth investors by promising—and consistently delivering—returns of 1 to 2 percent each month. It sounded too good to be true, but over many years Madoff delivered what he promised, so who could argue with the results?

It *was* too good to be true. In December 2008, Madoff's house of cards collapsed when federal officials arrested him for running an estimated $50 billion Ponzi scheme. His game: He never actually invested the principal entrusted to him. Instead, he used those funds to pay back other investors their promised interest.

His pyramid scam worked for decades because Madoff's never-fail reputation kept new capital coming. Some investors merely trusted his reputation and fell as innocent victims. A few savvy investors knew his numbers didn't add up, but chose to look the other way. The tempting payoff was too enticing.

In the end, Andrew's bill, like Madoff's and Puccini's, came due. Bills always do. Andrew hit bottom. His personal Ponzi scheme couldn't hide the fact that the garbage produced by his bad choices had to go somewhere.

"So why drugs? What pulled you in?" I asked Andrew.

"They feel good."

"But you quit," I said, admiring his honesty yet wondering what inner Rubicon he'd crossed to conquer his crisis. Andrew, like all of us, was an instinctive mathematician. He'd figured out that the algebraic scales of the world must balance.

Andrew leaned back, took a deep breath, and stirred like he was about to call it quits. He looked back over his shoulder and spotted his mother still sitting in the back.

He broke the silence randomly: "I grew up coming to a church like this, except we sang songs out of hymnbooks. I felt embarrassed being a Christian. Homophobia, the Crusades, all that. In high school I started using drugs. They took me somewhere religion never did. I never met a Christian who seemed to have a pulse." He paused and looked at me. I thought about checking mine.

"But last year the drugs got crazy. I started stealing stuff and I got caught. I knew I needed help. My mother tried to send me to Teen Challenge. I knew people who'd been through it. Way too Holy Roller for me. I went to Horizon instead."

"Did Horizon help?"

"Saved my life."

"How?" I'd heard secondhand about this treatment program. I was genuinely curious.

"You ever heard of Anthony Robbins?"

"I have," I said. "In fact, I went to high school with him, but that's another story. . . ."

"Really? What do you think of his stuff?"

"Some of it is good; some is nonsense; some, I think, is dangerous."

"It worked for me," Andrew said. I sensed him closing off again.

"How?" I was now truly hoping to keep the conversation going.

"He taught me techniques to condition my mind and emotions, like Pavlov's dog. I used to blow up like a volcano. Someone would say something stupid and I'd explode.

Robbins showed me how to install good responses, like tranquillity, so that when someone presses my button, peace comes out instead of anger. Everyone gets manipulated by things, even you." Andrew said this and waited for me to respond. I didn't. So he went on. "Instead of letting things happen to me, I can engineer my own instincts. Robbins calls it the Dickens Pattern—finding leverage strong enough to force genuine transformation, like the ghosts used on Ebenezer Scrooge."

"So that's how you broke the grip of drugs? You Scrooged yourself by looking at your Christmas future on drugs?"

"Basically. I mean, it was part of the answer for me. It helped."

I could sense an underlying uncertainty. I understood the Robbins' approach. The temptation to seek one silver bullet, one magical solution. Andrew had first tried to ignore Karma. Here he'd tried some magic to make it disappear. Robbins' techniques promise simple solutions to deeply complex problems, and frankly, they don't deliver all the magic they promise.

We love the thought of magic. Gino Castignoli lived through decades of heartbreak before his beloved Red Sox finally overcame the Curse of the Bambino to win the 2004 World Series. He thought he'd die of cardiac arrest in 1975, when the Cincinnati Reds scored a run in the top of the ninth of game seven to beat the Sox. Then there was the bitter humiliation of 1986, the Mets' improbable comeback and the grounder between Bill Buckner's wobbling wickets. But now that the Sox had broken through the curse they'd suffered since trading Babe Ruth to the Yankees, he wanted to ensure they would remain winners.

So when Castignoli joined the construction crew pouring concrete for the site of the new Yankee Stadium, he conceived a plan: he would implant a little memento to give the Yankees, the Sox's archrival, a little taste of their own magic. As wet concrete flowed into one of the footings of the stadium, Castignoli discreetly tossed something into the mix. That something was a Red Sox slugger David Ortiz game-used jersey. Castignoli wanted the foundation of the new Yankee Stadium to play eternal host to a uniform worn by the hero who had led Sox fans out of the wilderness of futility. In baseball, symbolism is substance. Such an offering to the gods of baseball would surely erode the Yankee mystique!

His co-workers thought so too. As fate would have it, someone in the crew—a Yankees' fan—witnessed Castignoli's sabotage and reported it. Later, armed with jackhammers and flanked by a battalion of reporters, Yankee officials ceremoniously exhumed Ortiz's jersey and then auctioned it off for charity.

Maybe most of us wouldn't go to such extremes, but odds are we're more superstitious than we want to admit. Eighty percent of Americans have played a lottery at least once, though statistically we're more likely to discover buried treasure in our backyard than pick a winning Lotto number. A researcher in England found that 86 percent of his fellow Brits practice "good luck" behavior such as knocking on wood, crossing fingers, avoiding walking under a ladder or breaking a mirror, carrying a good luck charm, and steering clear of the number thirteen. Given the stakes and our powerlessness to fix our Karma, we're prone to try anything to gain an upper hand. Andrew had tried the simplistic classical conditioning triggers of Tony Robbins. He said they'd helped, but I doubted he had as much confidence as he professed. Magic formulas seldom give fixed, permanent confidence.

"Have you ever heard of Eckhart Tolle?" Andrew added.

"I have."

"Horizon uses Tolle too," he said. "From Tolle I learned to free myself from dread of the future and regret of the past. He's big on the power of *now*. He says we must release desires that make us discontented. Tolle believes that peace comes when we stop trying to be ourselves, stop wanting things, and instead release ourselves to whatever is."

"Sounds like the teachings of the Buddha."

"Exactly!" Andrew said.

"Sounds opposite to Robbins."

"Things can be opposite and still true. Opposites balance. One of the guys in my group discussion said that he thought Christianity was dying and would be gone in a generation. The director said he didn't think so. He said he thought that everything is coming together. Christianity isn't dying—it's melting back into its esoteric roots, where it will be balanced by its opposites like Buddhism. Buddha lived before Jesus, you know. Most of what Jesus said he got from Buddha."

"Not so. But that's another discussion. So how did Tolle help you actually break the grip of drugs?"

"He gave me practical actions to follow," Andrew explained. "You've heard about *The Secret* and the law of attraction?"

I nodded.

"We get whatever we want. Like attracts like. It's the most ancient wisdom we have. If I am kind, I draw kindness back. Once I saw this, I just had to decide if I wanted good things or bad things coming back to me. I had the power to make my destiny. As long as I did drugs and all the garbage that goes with it, that's all I could expect back. I decided I wanted something else. I started *acting* free. I quit."

A couple of lingering spectators edged closer to catch a snippet of our conversation. Andrew either didn't notice or he didn't care.

"So you're fixed. . . . You've changed yourself for good?" I asked him, recognizing in his progression the third typical solution we humans attempt in our efforts to "dump" our Karma: raw brute force, the "buck up" system of success. "Do you have any fear that your changes won't last?"

"I'm changed," he said flatly.

I couldn't help but think about my own recent New Year's resolutions. It was only February and I'd faded fast! Our Western New Year's, coming as it does in the dead of winter, seems to offer a parabolic opportunity to decide for change just when things look darkest: lose weight, quit nagging, read more books, finish writing this book. We promise ourselves what we wish could be. "Henceforth," we vow, "things shall be different." And with those words we draw a line in the sand and step across.

What could be easier?

The problem is most resolutions don't work. I can attest. According to recent research, 67 percent of Americans make more than one resolution, and 70 percent fail on their first attempt. Evidently, wishing doesn't make it so.

The week I outlined this chapter, I went with my twenty-one-year-old daughter, Emily, to see a stage production of Shakespeare's *Macbeth*—a quintessential tale of the futility of humans attempting to engineer destiny, then clean up the toxic mess strewn in the process.

At the beginning of the drama, Lady Macbeth has no conscience. She coldly manipulates her husband to kill King Duncan and lay hold of the royal destiny prophesied for him. When Macbeth balks at her plot, she mocks his cowardliness, and even his manhood. Her cold-blooded determination and icy will make her one of the darkest villains in all of literature.

But after the murder, Macbeth and his wife seem to trade souls. Macbeth grows cold and calculating; his lady begins suffocating from guilt. She grows obsessed with a compulsion to cleanse her hands of the crime. "Out, damned spot! Out, I say!" she wails as she attempts to wash the stain away. Her efforts at self-atonement fail. In the end, she goes mad with regret. Unable to dispose of her guilt, she kills herself in judgment on her own iniquity.

Self-atonement always fails. We cannot wash away our own shame. Having learned this by trial and error, humans have invented other remedies, the likes of which fall under the broad-brush label *spiritual*.

Saul of Tarsus seemed to understand this about his own history. Saul became a professional religious do-gooder at an early age. As a top-of-the-class graduate of the school of Pharisaical religiosity run by Rabbi Gamaliel, the grandson of Hillel, one of the fathers of the Pharisaic religious party, Saul had a pretty clear idea of what was and wasn't expected of him—and of everyone else. Like the rest of the Pharisees, Saul understood his role: He was a living conscience for the nation of Israel, making sure that no one veered from the path of legal rightness.

The Pharisees believed that the tragedies in Israel's past happened because Israel ignored moral standards. Pharisees wanted to ensure Israel never again suffered devastation, so they set up a meticulous scorecard for individual behavior. Pharisees were the moral police of their day.

And no one showed more zeal for the mission than young Saul. When a group of Jews began proclaiming that belief in Jesus, a supposed prophet who had been executed by the Romans, offered a "free gift of righteousness" to everyone who believed, Saul went ballistic in a violent campaign to stamp out the heresy and the heretics.

But then something happened to Saul. He later claimed that he personally encountered Jesus in a supernatural moment that quite literally left him blind. In the process of a miraculous recovery, Saul became a believer in Jesus as he also came face-to-face with his own moral futility. As a Pharisee, he had focused on behavior as a moral barometer. Encountering Jesus, he realized he had "acted" morally, but had remained enslaved to powerful immoral inclinations. He could never be truly good enough for God. Meeting Jesus awakened a deeper conscience and a helpless doom. The harder Saul worked to clear his own name, the more guilt he uncovered. He could never work his way to goodness.

In a famous letter to fellow Jesus-followers in Rome, Paul (he changed his name when he changed loyalties) poured out a confession of his helplessness:

> I have discovered this principle of life—that when I want to do what is right, I inevitably do what is wrong. I love God's law with all my heart. But there is another power within me that is at war with my mind. This power makes me a slave to the sin that is still within me. Oh, what a miserable person I am! Who will free me from this life that is dominated by sin and death?

The Law of God, Paul says, gives form to our own innate conscience. Everyone knows what is right and wrong because God has put that knowledge deep within us. In our conscience, God communicates what he does and doesn't wish for us. The legal code articulates this intuitive standard. The problem is no person, no matter how hard he or she works, can fulfill these standards of right and wrong. We might fight to act in the right way, but we can never tame our motives.

Paul understood this more than most. And he knew he could never run faster than his guilt. He burned up his early years trying to live perfectly, and came away feeling futile and helpless and in need of another solution for true change. Paul found his answer in Jesus' ability to change him.

Perhaps like Paul we're all doomed to fail in our efforts to free ourselves.

I clipped another humorous news story as an allegorical case in point: Eighteen months into a life sentence for first-degree murder, James Leroy Scott, an inmate in Minnesota's Stillwater Prison, had had enough. He plotted an escape—and nearly succeeded.

Working for months while other prisoners slept, Scott managed to hack through two sets of steel bars, cut through a fence, scale a roof, commandeer power tools from a workshop, and scrounge enough wood to construct a twenty-foot platform that would have reached over the prison wall. To mask his absence from his cell, Scott stuffed his bunk with pillows and clothing, and even positioned a fan to rustle the blankets and mimic his breathing.

But in the end, Scott's genius failed him when he discovered that the platform he'd built proved too heavy to move.

Too exhausted to continue, Scott gave up and rang a loading dock bell, just a few feet short of his goal. When guards arrived at 5:15 AM on May 19, he confessed everything. "I got out of the doghouse, tried to escape, it didn't work."

It never really does. Escaping is exhausting business, and in the end, impossible. When we hit our moral bankruptcy and realize we cannot, on our own, outrun the consequences of choices, we have four options: (1) we can deny the crisis; (2) we can attempt a bit of magic; (3) we can scramble back to our feet looking for one more loophole; or (4) we can concede the case and throw ourselves at the mercy of the judge.

Most of us choose anything but the last option.

"I have to keep moving," Andrew admitted.

"Resolution might take a long time, maybe a very, very long time."

"Well, working things out doesn't have to stop when our heart stops. Eighty years is probably far too short a time to set everything straight," he said.

"So there's your caveat: You can just live through as many lifetimes as it takes until you finally find the way to neutralize negative Karma. A life precedes you; another life will succeed you, is that right?"

"It is," Andrew said, and he suddenly sounded like a wise and tempered sage. "Birth is not the beginning; death not the end. They are each just chapter headings in a longer story. Work has been going on; work will continue. Every person's Karma story stretches back and forward beyond the scope of the few years we call this life. I'm small potatoes."

I thought again of E. Stanley Jones' discussions. In the end, if our efforts to ignore Karma or magically and religiously make it disappear, or adding and subtracting by sheer effort don't fix it, we have to resort to deferring justice out into the future, maybe even a very distant future. The Hindus and Buddhists around Jones' Round Table all eventually fell back to this position.

"So we can keep living and fighting forever? Seems like just a long deferment, like the government loading their spent nuclear fuel onto a semitrailer, driving it around for fifty years, and calling that their solution to toxic waste."

"Like it or not, Karma is," he said.

"I guess I buy that," I admitted. "But for the record, I don't take the reincarnation rider that goes along with it. I think there's a better solution. But for what it's worth, sure, justice wins in the end—which is why we're all doomed."

"You can't change the rules just because you don't like the score of the game," Andrew quipped.

"I agree. I'm just pointing out the problem Karma creates. In the end, we all get what's coming, and what's coming is not all nice. What am I gonna do when the garbage of my lifetime gets dumped on my doorstep?" I asked.

"I know where you're headed. Your trump card—forgiveness. That's what bugs me about your religion—it's a cheap way out," Andrew snapped. "Say the wonder words of your sinner's prayer; go for a little swim in a dunk tank; chew on some stale bread and down a shot of cheap wine, and presto, I don't have to worry anymore about how I shafted my roommate. I'm forgiven—whatever that means. That sounds more like magic to me than Anthony Robbins."

"What you're saying is that negative consequences have to be paid for. We can't just invent new rules, wave a wand,

and pretend causes can dodge effects, *and* that I don't have to give an account as a result. Right?"

"Sure." He nodded.

"Then I agree with you. Because the stuff has to go somewhere."

"So," Andrew smirked. "Maybe you don't believe in forgiveness. . . ."

5

WEB OF INTRIGUE

"Believe in forgiveness? I depend on it," I replied.

"Yeah, what's the worst thing you've ever done?" Andrew shot back. "I'll bet you were the teacher's pet. You've never pushed the line on anything worse than 45 in a 35-mile-per-hour zone."

"You might be surprised. Okay . . . I already said I've never killed anyone. But evil comes in many packages. If Karma keeps score, I'm bankrupt."

"What specifically?" He waited, like a priest behind a screen.

I brushed the tip of my nose with the back of my hand and caught the faint whiff of hand sanitizer I'd used in the hospital that afternoon. An image of my father lying motionless again invaded my thoughts. Had I owned up to all the petty wounds I'd inflicted on him, the kinds a son can deliver in the hand-to-hand sparring that flares up when we invade one another's worlds? I felt no twinge in my conscience. Regret, maybe, but no unresolved guilt. The slate was clean, thank God!

Then I caught hold of a hint of buried resentment and recognized the taste. As foolish and selfish and irrational as it seemed, and as embarrassing as it is to admit, I knew I felt angry that my father had left us in this disarray. He didn't choose this stroke. I knew that. And he would have hated knowing he'd caused us pain. Still, I knew I needed to release him, forgive him for the burden his sudden sickness had imposed.

Imposition.

My Great Uncle Cecil hated to impose on people. He'd go to any length to avoid having to put anyone out. Example: Years ago we lived a mile from Cecil, and one evening my father stopped by for a visit and found him sprawled on his couch utterly exhausted.

"Hey, Cec, you look spent. What'd you do today?" my father asked as he stuck his head in the front door.

"Oh, went down to Long Beach to pick up my Chevy."

"Who drove you?"

"Nobody," said Cecil sheepishly.

"Then how'd you get down there?"

"I drove my Dodge," Cec answered.

"Then how'd you get back?" My dad looked out in the driveway and saw both of Cecil's cars. "So you drove your Dodge to pick up your Chevy . . . by yourself?"

"Uh-huh," he said, avoiding eye contact.

"How'd you get both cars back?" my father asked directly, with something between irritation and perplexed bewilderment. Cecil was in his mid-sixties at the time and whatever he'd done, it had been physically costly.

Cecil was quiet. My father waited. Finally the story came. "Well, I didn't want to put anybody out. And Howard, I know you're busy . . . I drove both cars back myself."

My father turned away to bury a rising tide of laughter. Slowly the picture was becoming clear.

"I drove the Dodge down and parked it a mile north of the repair shop. Then I walked the rest of the way, paid for the Chevy—I blew a head gasket while I was down there last week—then I drove it a mile past the Dodge. I walked back, drove the Dodge a mile past the Chevy and . . . Well, you get the idea."

My father stood there speechless; then despite his best efforts, the dam broke. He burst out laughing in a fit so hard he nearly lost consciousness. The thought of a sixty-year-old man leapfrogging his way fifty miles was more than he could bear. "Well, how do you feel, you old fool?"

"I'm pretty tuckered out," Cec admitted.

"I wonder why! And all because you didn't want to ask for help. Thing is, Cec, now you're gonna be sore all week, and I'm gonna have to come over and mow your lawn. So you're putting me out one way if not another! If you don't beat all!"

We all impose one way or another. Karma is never purely personal because human life is not lived purely personally.

Clipping from Portland *Oregonian*, May 30, 2002, Mount Hood, Oregon: A disaster began with one mountain climber and one misstep. Perhaps his crampon gave way in the ice, or a rock broke loose, or a gust of wind tipped his balance. No one knows for sure. Whatever began the accident, it triggered a freakish chain of events that took the lives of three climbers and injured twelve.

It happened east of Portland on an icy ledge just below the summit of the ancient volcano that rises 11,240 feet. One of four climbers lost his grip on the slope. When he fell, he pulled his roped-together partners with him. Their rope snagged two other climbing groups and ripped them off the mountain as well.

KFSN-TV story from November 3, 2007, Clovis, California: Morris Earl Taylor had a blood-alcohol level of .24 percent—three times the legal limit—when he rear-ended a van, then lost control of his vehicle in a bank of dense fog. Two seconds later a second car hit Taylor's. Then another slammed into that vehicle, then another, and another. . . . A chain-reaction disaster followed. Ninety seconds later more than one hundred cars had crashed on Highway 99 just south of Fresno. The accident became the worst multi-car pileup in central California history. Two people were killed and dozens sustained injuries.

Clipping from the *New York Times,* November 28, 2008, Long Island, New York: The crowd of would-be Wal-Mart bargain hunters had grown throughout the night into a throng of two thousand stretching across the parking lot of the Green Acres Mall.

As the 5:00 AM opening for the day-after-Thanksgiving sale neared, the mob suddenly began to move en masse. Tension mounted. Fists began to pound and shoulders press against the sliding-glass double doors. Suddenly, bowed from the weight of the mob, the doors shattered and the shrieking mass surged through, all in a rush to get a deal on a TV or a computer.

Jdimytai Damour, a Wal-Mart employee, had attempted to guard the entrance. He was hurled down and trampled in the stampede. Other Wal-Mart workers pressed through to help him but were too late. When the crowd had finally passed through into the store, Mr. Damour lay dead.

The police officer in charge of the investigation called the scene "utter chaos." But even with evidence from surveillance videos, he acknowledged it would be difficult to identify the particular individuals responsible.

Conclusion: Not only do I have to worry about my own bad Karma, I have to worry about my neighbor and the stranger I've never met. I can climb ever so carefully, drive flawlessly, and diligently fulfill my own responsibilities. No matter. One slipup and down falls a whole line of chained-together relationships.

"I'll tell you what I did. I promise," I said. "But first"—I tried to frame this carefully—"you've reaped what you've sown. Have you reaped some of what others have sown? And have others been impacted by your choices?"

Andrew glanced back toward his mother. "Duh," he answered.

"We're not masters of our own destiny," I said. "Karma passes from one person to another like the swine flu in a packed elevator. I didn't ask for some of what I've caught, but I caught it nonetheless. And I know I've given my share of trouble to people who didn't deserve it too."

I understood even then, before I did research for this book, that I was spouting heresy from the perspective of

Dharmic religions like Hinduism, Buddhism, and the New
Age. These systems believe that anything bad in life comes
because at some time—perhaps in a past incarnation—I
planted seeds that have now sprouted. I asked for it. *Personal* justice will track me down like a relentless posse, even
through time. Victimhood doesn't exist. I'm always and
fully culpable.

My own religious tradition explains suffering and justice differently. Ancient Judaism, the root of Christianity,
believes that the effects of causes can travel through time
as well. But this line isn't entirely personal. In place of reincarnation, which attaches justice to an individual, Hebrew
tradition calls it retribution and tracks it down generation
lines, parent to child, to grandchild, to great-grandchild.
Parents' choices impact their own destiny *and* the destinies
of their children, and their children's children. Pain in
the world is a compounded, chaotic, interlaced wad of foul
human choices traceable back through many generations.
The second of the Ten Commandments puts it this way:

> You must not make for yourself an idol of any kind or
> an image of anything in the heavens or on the earth or
> in the sea. You must not bow down to them or worship
> them, for I, the Lord your God, am a jealous God who
> will not tolerate your affection for any other gods. I lay
> the sins of the parents upon their children; the entire
> family is affected—even children in the third and fourth
> generations of those who reject me. But I lavish unfailing
> love for a thousand generations on those who love me
> and obey my commands.

For Jews (and later for Christians), the consequences
of iniquity and the blessings of goodness do not jump

incarnations, they follow down relationship lines. Redemption, when and if it comes, must therefore answer personal and collective sins.

Jewish and Christian literature takes this theme of generational blessing and cursing very seriously. God promises Abraham that his family will receive special favor because Abraham remained faithful to him. This promise does happen. Abraham's son Isaac seems to have his father's "golden touch." Favor follows down the line. But Isaac also inherits his father's brand of fear and a propensity to lie to save his skin. Both Abraham and Isaac tell lies to a powerful king, claiming their wives are their sisters. So does a son inherit a tendency to lie as much as he inherits eye color and diabetes?

David receives a promise similar to Abraham. God tells him his descendants will sit on Israel's throne because David had shown himself a man who ran after God with all his heart. But David's children also suffer the dire consequences of their father's sexual sins—his tendency to run with all his heart after another man's wife. This root of perversion eroded peace from the lives of David's children.

An ancient Jewish proverb put it this way:

> The parents have eaten sour grapes,
>   but their children's mouths pucker at the taste.

I abbreviated this idea for Andrew: "I suffer for my own lousy choices," I said. "So too will my children, and my friends, and the stranger driving the car beside me if I forget to look in the mirror before changing lanes. We're impacted by others. My father, for instance, may be dying today—"

"Sorry," Andrew interjected.

"It's okay. But I'm living in the crosswinds of his powerful life. That's mostly good, but there's no denying the weight of the gravity of his presence and now his sickness. I suppose the generations that follow me will inherit whatever ripples I make too. That's a sobering prospect. But that's how Christians see the interdependence of our relationships. Karma is complicated because nature is complicated, and because what happens in other people's worlds crashes over into mine."

As I said this, I had a thought. If Karma can be passed by accident, can it also be passed on purpose, by deliberate intent? Can good will be voluntarily transferred and credited to another? At the time I had no idea how Eastern religions would answer this, though I suspected it wouldn't be the same answer I claimed as a Christian. Later in my reading, I found some surprises.

Some Buddhist teaching about Karma includes a clause called "transfer of merit." Good deeds and the benefits associated with them and their consequences belong, by the laws of the universe, to those who perform them. But in some cases, these credits can be relinquished and shared with others if those who "own" them willingly release them. Buddhist monks, for instance, through their dedication to an ascetic life, supposedly store up extra "good Karma" and can then debit their own ledger and credit it back to their ancestors whom they believe to be bound in endless cycles of reincarnation. Leftover blessings, like leftover tomatoes from the garden, get passed along.

This concept strikes a remarkably similar tone to the Catholic doctrine of the "treasury of merit." This teaching claims that the sum total of all the goodness of Jesus, Mary, and the saints has so enriched the heavenly family of God that these overflowing riches can be generously shared with others who may not yet possess enough personal virtue to warrant salvation. In the Middle Ages the church marketed indulgences, a kind of stock certificate that gave their possessors a claim to a specified amount of "merit" stored in the vaults of heaven. Indulgences could be purchased not only for personal use, but for those already dead and trapped in Purgatory.

Esoteric doctrines like the "treasury of merit" and "transfer of merit" are religions' attempts at a kind of spiritual leap year, added in to balance the equation when pure algebra doesn't work—the way Einstein introduced his "cosmological constant" in order to make his own math work to prove his theories.

But then another question must follow. If credit for good deeds and their favorable consequences can (perhaps) be swapped from one person to another, what about blame, and the consequences for blame, and bad choices in general? Can they transfer as well? Can *suffering* be voluntarily carried by one person for another?

Perhaps you see where this is leading. Baseball!

It's a stretch during a long Minnesota winter to imagine the magical wonder of baseball. But it happened: Carrying another's suffering reminded me of sacrifice; sacrifice reminded me of baseball, and baseball of W. P. Kinsella's novel *Shoeless Joe* and the film *Field of Dreams* based on it.

Shoeless Joe, laced with strange and mystical overtones, begins when an Iowa farmer named Ray Kinsella hears a voice whisper, "If you build it, he will come." After several such encounters, Ray takes the voice seriously and complies: He builds a baseball field in his cornfield.

Many do come. Great baseball ghosts from the past walk out from the cornstalks in left field and play ball under the lights long into the summer nights. Among them, the great Shoeless Joe Jackson and other members of the "Black Sox" team, banned from baseball for throwing the 1919 World Series, and Archibald "Moonlight" Graham, whose career ended before he ever got to bat in a major league game.

Ray hears the voice again: "Ease his pain," it says. Ray sets out to discover what this means, and in a series of strange twists, ends up traveling across the country to find the reclusive writer and baseball fan J. D. Salinger.

The story climaxes when John Kinsella, Ray's deceased father, appears on the ball field. John had played minor league baseball, but his life ended in disappointment. Shoeless Joe approaches Ray to thank him for making this "miracle" possible. Joe points to John, Ray's father. It becomes clear to Ray that he is the one in the promise, "If you build it, he will come." By easing the pain of others, Ray himself finds meaning and fulfillment.

Shoeless Joe hints at one of the great themes in literature—the vicarious suffering of one person for another. Other great writers hit this theme square on the mark.

The Russians have a proclivity for true heroic suffering both in their history and in their literature. Leo Tolstoy, in *War and Peace*, relays the story of a merchant sentenced to prison in Siberia for a murder he didn't commit. Years later, the merchant meets the guilty man and claims that he has been suffering for the man's sins. The merchant has not only taken up the punishment, he has become the sin itself.

Dostoevsky's *Crime and Punishment* tells the story of Mikolka, who is mistakenly arrested for the murder of two women, who were actually killed by a man named Raskolnikov. Mikolka, who originally intended to live an ascetic life, had recently fallen into a life of debauchery. After his arrest, he decides to redeem himself through suffering and confesses to the crime he did not commit. Petrovich, the detective in charge of the case, does not believe Mikolka, yet he delays arresting Raskolnikov, hoping he will repent. He does not. Raskolnikov feels no guilt for his crime. The story is a bitter tragedy of the real weight and cost of substitutionary suffering.

Others have given the exchange of suffering an actual, almost magical power to lift away suffering. Is it possible for one to actually carry another's pain?

In Rudyard Kipling's short story "The Wish House," the widow Grace Ashcroft explains to her childhood friend Mrs. Fettley the origin of the debilitating ulcer on her shin. During a visit to the country, Grace falls deeply in love with a man named Harry Mockler. Eventually Harry leaves Grace, and when they later meet by chance, Harry appears physically broken after a bout with blood poisoning.

Grace is heartbroken. She travels to London to a "Wish House"—the haunt of a wraith or "Token" that can grant a person's wish to take up another person's trouble. Grace "wishes" to take upon herself "everything bad that's in store for my man, 'Arry Mockler, for love's sake."

It works, evidently. Soon after, Grace injures her ankle and then develops a nasty boil on her leg. It grows worse whenever Harry is ill or in trouble and finally turns into a painful cancer.

As Mrs. Fettley sets to leave, Grace says, "But the pain do count, don't ye think, Liz? The pain do count to keep 'Arry—where I want 'im." And where does she want him? Unmarried and living with his mother. Clearly Grace Ashcroft's desire to carry Harry's suffering comes not from pure love, but from a kind of fierce, possessive obsession to control and own him.

The British writer Charles Williams, listed among the Oxford "Inklings"—the writer's club attended by, among others, J. R. R. Tolkien and C. S. Lewis—developed this concept into something close to religious doctrine. Williams evidently took the theory quite literally and spoke openly of its power. In his novel *Descent Into Hell*, Williams puts this idea to the test with a story of one character trapped by a paralyzing fear.

In Battle Hill, a community just north of London, a local drama group stages a play by the distinguished playwright and poet Peter Stanhope. One of the actors, Pauline Anstruther, believes she is being pursued by a doppelganger, a type of ghost that approaches her whenever she is alone. As a result, Pauline lives in almost constant terror.

Sensing her crisis, Stanhope introduces Pauline to the miracle of substitution: the gift of one person taking up the burdens of another person. Stanhope offers to take Pauline's fear for her. He tells her that the next time she experiences fear she must imagine him standing in her place, then allow him to feel the fear for her. Stanhope then explains how he will likewise visualize her situation and open himself completely to emotions similar to hers. He comforts her by admitting that the weight for him will be lighter because he holds no deep attachment or history in it.

When Pauline next experiences dread, she does imagine releasing her fears to Stanhope, and he in turn absorbs that fear. The process works. Pauline finds deliverance, and along the way discovers that the ghost she has fled for so long is actually her ideal spiritual self.

Does this theme reappear so often in literature because we somehow perceive it as something real for real life?

Perhaps. Some have actually experimented with this principle and lived to tell about it.

One of Charles Williams' close friends, renowned writer and philosopher C. S. Lewis, lived a peaceful bachelor's life until he began corresponding with an American poet named Joy Gresham. Her warm and bold candor, her familiarity with Lewis's thought and work, and her willingness—and ability—to banter playfully with him finally enticed him to meet her. A remarkable friendship followed.

Upon her return to America, Gresham's husband divorced her for another woman. Joy and her sons then moved to England, where she and Lewis continued to cultivate their friendship. When Joy learned that British immigration denied her permission to remain in the country, Lewis offered to help—by marrying her. With marriage license in hand, she was granted admittance.

But not long after their "official" marriage, and just as Lewis began to sense a genuine love growing for her, Joy was diagnosed with terminal cancer. Brokenhearted, Lewis came to her bedside, announced his love, and asked for her hand in true marriage. There in the hospital they were joined in Christian marriage.

Lewis then took a drastic step. No doubt influenced by Williams, Lewis prayed that he might take up and bear Joy's pain. Nevill Coghill, a friend of Lewis, remembered what happened next.

> This was a power which Lewis found himself later to possess, and which, he told me, he had been allowed to use to ease the suffering of his wife, a cancer victim, of whom the doctors had despaired. . . . "You mean," I said, "that her pain left her, and that you felt it for her in your body?" "Yes," he said, "in my legs. It was crippling. But it relieved hers."

The Russian novels, Rudyard Kipling, and C. S. Lewis faded to gray, and I returned to thinking again about Shoeless Joe and my own vivid memories of playing catch with my dad, much as Ray had with his. I learned to love the game all on my own, but my father put the ball and bat in my hands and a Giants cap on my head. My later brazen rebellion of becoming a Dodgers fan notwithstanding, we always shared baseball down to the core of our collective soul. That night I groped again for a way that I might "ease his pain" or that someone else might ease mine.

Pain, of course, cannot magically disappear. But evidently it can be miraculously moved. Sorrow may pass to another by accident, or it may move by permission, and then be carried as the hard price of love. Either way, humans seem fully capable of sharing one another's destinies.

Ancient cultures had a word to define what happens when two people exchange the just outcomes of one another's lives. They called it a covenant.

The story of David and Jonathan, preserved in the ancient Hebrew texts, depicts the amazing power and mystery of covenant.

Prince Jonathan, the son of Israel's King Saul, held a hereditary right to the throne. His father, Saul, had lost legitimacy because of treason. Some of his actions even suggested insanity. Israel needed a new king.

Israel's seer, a wise sage named Samuel, recognized the problem. After searching through the realm, he identified an unlikely successor, a young boy named David, the youngest son of a shepherd named Jesse. Samuel ceremoniously poured oil over David's head and declared the lad the intended king of Israel. The kingdom would be torn away from Saul and his family and be given to David.

Saul did not take kindly to this coup, and set out to destroy David. In fact, he chased David for years looking for an opportunity to kill him. Jonathan, however, did not share his father's jealousy. Though he had a great deal to lose should the monarchy move from Saul's line to David's, Jonathan responded with stunning graciousness. He affirmed David's appointment and vowed his support, and he offered a *covenant* promise as a pledge.

Covenants have miraculous power. But what is a covenant?

Halvor Nelson can do just about anything. After years as an executive with a multinational corporation, Halvor had had enough of the tension and hassles of managing troublesome people. He quit and gave himself a promotion: He started working as a handyman for hapless homeowners—like me. Trained originally as an electrical engineer, Halvor has always had an astounding work ethic. He still works sixty hours a week, but now he's doing what he really loves . . . fixing clogged drains, installing new garage-door openers, rewiring out-of-code fuse boxes. We call Halvor a couple of times a month for this or that. He's prompt and efficient, and he charges a reasonable fee. That's our relationship with him: He replaces the broken garbage disposal, and we pay him for his trouble.

But as reliable as Halvor may be, his relationship with our family has limits. Sometimes if he's around while we're eating dinner or lunch, my wife, Jill, will offer something to him. Sometimes he'll agree. But we'd probably not invite him for Thanksgiving, and he probably wouldn't accept if we did. Our obligation to him and his to us is contractual, simple, straightforward, and limited: He stops the leak, and I pay him forty dollars. Our relationship goes no further than fee-for-service.

Covenants are different arrangements. Like contracts, they define relationships with stipulations, a promise with a promise. But while a contract exchanges like for like or like value for like value of items, a covenant exchanges much more. Covenants offer life for a life and destiny for a destiny. To be in covenant with someone is to offer everything, and claim everything.

Covenants are rare these days. Marriage is perhaps the last such arrangement in our culture. But covenants were common in the ancient world. Two kings might strike a deal and exchange loyalties with each other, often offering their daughters in marriage as a pledge of the depth of their commitment. Kings would also offer covenants to their citizens, promising protection and provision in exchange for loyalty. They could make a covenant with conquered foes, offering mercy even when their defeated enemies could offer nothing of value in return. Merchants would make covenants with other merchants. Friends would stipulate the nature of their relationships. These formal exchanges stood permanently; they were comprehensive, and deadly serious.

Covenants, as unique as the people and situations making them, all shared a similar pattern. A formal covenant would typically involve a ceremony in which those convening the relationship would make public declarations before witnesses and record them in a written document. This process would include:

- An introduction of the parties
- A retelling of the history of their relationship
- Stipulations in the covenant
- A public declaration that this was now a reality
- Signing this agreement before the witnesses
- Pronouncing the blessings and curses associated with the relationship: blessings if the covenant stipulations were kept and curses if they were not
- A feast to consummate the arrangement.

Within these binding arrangements, relationships became predictable. Everyone involved in a covenant knows precisely what is expected of them and what they can expect from their partners in return. People in ancient cultures found this formality quite normal. In fact, they were friends with others not because they liked each other. They were friends because they had built a base of confidence on a promise that allowed them to trust. In a covenant, two parties would trade destinies. They joined their souls, their lives, their Karma.

David received Jonathan's friendship, and the two forged a covenant. In their mutual pledge, they in essence traded destinies. Jonathan's "Karma" became David's—he became the new prince and the rightful heir to the throne. Jonathan in return received David's natural role of servant. This willing exchange stands as one of the most magnanimous expressions of graciousness in history. One life impacted another.

I lowered my eyes. A dark and shameful memory came rising up from subterranean realms. The pit of my stomach said, *Tell him.*

Andrew studied me closely. I cleared my throat and told him my confession within this story:

Somewhere a woman named Roxanne might be sitting alone at night trying to silence the voices in her head. One of those voices is mine. I no longer know where she lives. I don't know if she beats her children, cuts herself, drinks vodka for breakfast, or writes hateful e-mails to advice columnists. I wouldn't be surprised at anything of the sort. I wouldn't be surprised at something worse.

I have not seen Roxanne since a clear, crisp Friday afternoon in March 1974, when she stepped off our school bus for the last time, the day she left our school. I drove her away.

I never intended to hurt Roxanne. We were bumbling through eighth grade at Soulsbyville School in the Gold Rush country east of Sonora, California. Roxanne had a disability. Her right hand hung at her side and she walked with a limp. She had large, beautiful sad eyes, and she seldom spoke. We rode the same bus every morning and afternoon forty minutes each way, weaving in and out of the little valleys where hearty and reclusive Californians had

tucked away their homes. I got bored on those long drives.
Generally, when I get bored I make trouble.

I grew up in a family of teasers. My father, who had the
kindest of hearts, loved to raise reactions with little ornery
jests. I learned early that affection comes with a jab and a
snicker. Herringshaws give this kind of attention. We tease.

I remember feeling uncomfortable with Roxanne's
sullen silence. She would sit in her seat alone, coddling
her useless hand, looking guarded and suspicious, staring
out the window at the green and rocky hills of Tuolumne
County. No one spoke much to Roxanne. She said even less.
I remember thinking she needed attention. I decided to
give her some. I started to joke with her.

I gave her a nickname that I can't recall now. I sat near
her whenever I could and peppered her with playful banter.
She'd tell me, beg me, to leave her alone, but her rebuffs
only made me more resolved. I know now—and probably
knew then—that some of my barbs crossed the line into
meanness, some even to abuse. But no one corrected me,
and I never corrected myself.

Then one day Roxanne stopped riding the bus. Her
parents removed her from the school and she disappeared
from my life.

At the time I didn't see a connection between my banter and her disappearance. I felt no responsibility. I never
intended to hurt anyone. It was all in good sport. But in
the years that followed, as my conscience and imagination matured, I sometimes played back the mental tape of
those bus rides and I saw clearly the brutality I had heaped
on Roxanne. I had not wanted to create pain. I had not
intended to chase her away. Yet that was the result. My
actions impacted her life.

Andrew nodded and studied me closely.

I added, "Others had probably added to her pain. But I'm an accomplice. I did this. If Karma matters and the universe recycles its justice, I'm damned."

"Okay. I get it," Andrew said. He looked at the floor. Then he looked up and caught my eye. "Man, that was evil."

"Yeah, I suppose. Unless there's an escape clause, it's bad news for me. What could I do in one lifetime to balance the scales?"

We sat silent for a moment, our eyes on the carpet. Then Andrew asked, with what I felt was real empathy, "How do you live with yourself?"

I looked back at him. "That's just it, Andrew. I don't have to. Forgiveness: I depend on it. Someone else eases my pain, and, I pray, hers as well."

A WORMHOLE INTO ETERNITY

"What if someone lived a perfect life?" I said this before realizing what I fully intended. *Could this pull things together?* I thought, as I listened to my own words. I went with my hunch and let it stand.

Andrew frowned. "A perfect life? What's that mean? After all you've said about unintended consequences, you ask this?"

"Theoretically, what Karma would follow a person who lived a perfect life?"

"I suppose they'd have perfect . . . Karma," Andrew answered cautiously.

My first faith crisis happened in a church; not my church, but a church nonetheless. I was ten or eleven years old, and my father and I had driven together from our home in Santa Cruz, California, to Oakland to take in a baseball game between the A's and the Orioles. Before the game, we stopped in at an Oakland church where a friend of my father served as pastor.

The building immediately felt familiar, like our church and others I'd visited. I recognized the midweek musty smell of an empty holy space. I'd never been there, yet I had.

My father's friend, a white-haired African-American man, thin as a rail and dressed in a black suit and tie, came out of his office to greet us. He hugged my father and they shared some inside joke and laughed for a while. Then the pastor looked me square in the eye, called me by name, which shocked me, and gave me a firm handshake. I sensed my father trusted him, so I decided I liked him as well.

Then the two men began talking. They served together on a committee of some sort and had business to cover. I stepped away and meandered down the hall and eventually into a library—walls lined with bookshelves, three old couches, a brick fireplace, and a prominent picture hanging above the mantel. The picture in that strange yet familiar place sent me tumbling into my first-ever faith crisis.

The scene it depicted seemed as ordinary as the moldy stuffiness of the room: A man in a white robe was smiling—it was obviously Jesus—and sitting on a large boulder, surrounded by children—some on his lap, some looking over his shoulder, some sitting politely at his feet. So familiar and yet so alien. In this picture Jesus was a black man, not just Jesus with dark skin. He clearly had the hair, mouth, and brow of an African-American. My immediate reaction was emotional. I think I laughed, and then felt strangely small and very out of place. What had they done to my Jesus?

My personal image of Jesus made sense. It came from storybooks we had at home and the print hanging above the fireplace in our congregation's library. In that painting Jesus stood in a boat tossing about in a storm, surrounded by his terrified disciples. That Jesus had a thin face, pale skin, and shoulder-length brown hair blowing in the wind. He looked, in fact, like our youth pastor, whom I idolized.

Standing there looking at a brown-skinned Jesus, I suddenly felt insecure and uncertain and lonely. And it wasn't the last time I felt this separation. The crisis hit again just two years ago when a friend showed me an article written by a team of forensic scientists who have built a composite of a face they claim represents a typical thirty-year-old male of Jesus' time and place. Jesus was, they contend, a first-century Jew from Palestine. Even given his purported miraculous conception, he still bore the DNA of his mother. This team studied skeletal remains of multiple individuals who lived in Israel at the time and from their observations developed their profile of a "typical" man.

When I first looked at the mockup, I went numb. It's Jesus as a Hezbollah terrorist! He looks—to me—angry, cold, anxious, and unpredictable. He seems alien, though I am culturally sensitive enough to realize most other Christians on the planet, those not of a northern European lineage, would not share my alienation. Nevertheless, I would still have a hard time sitting down next to *this* Jesus for a tender moment of communion with God.

Will the real Jesus please stand up! In Byzantine mosaics he holds his head like a nobleman from Constantinople. In Flemish paintings he looks like a Dutch trader. In twentieth-century films he comes off as a Hollywood hunk. Who's right? Is Jesus like me, or my father's friend, or a shopkeeper from the West Bank? Every culture wants a picture of God they can cherish. God created us in his image; do we also try to create God in ours? Who was—who is—Jesus of Nazareth?

"You think Jesus was a perfect human being." Andrew wasn't taking the bait.

"What do you think?" I asked.

"Good maybe. But perfect?"

"Actually maybe just the opposite."

Andrew sat back and crossed his arms.

"He could be perfect," I suggested, "but never merely good. He claimed perfection, not only by what he said, but in his actions. If he wasn't what he claimed, he was either a nutcase or a devious liar—anything but merely good."

"I'm not convinced there even was a historical person named Jesus. Or if there was, we don't know the truth about him. The documents about him are biased."

"It's easy to play cynic, Andrew. But follow that line of thought and you never have to answer any idea, just dismiss it. Yet in the end cynicism makes knowledge itself impossible. It turns every statement into someone's opinion. But then, even cynicism itself gets eroded. We can't live suspicious of everything. In order to think up cynicism, cynics have to assume their own reasoning. That's trust and faith. At some point we all have to take some piece of evidence at face value and build a life on that. I choose to accept the records of Jesus as reliable historical documents."

"What evidence?" Andrew folded his arms, but he still seemed honestly curious.

I thought for a moment, then reached into my satchel for a book I was reviewing called *Questions of Life* by Nicky Gumbel. Gumbel started the Alpha course, an introduction to Christianity, which began in Great Britain and has now grown around the world. In his book, Gumbel makes a succinct argument for the reliability of the accounts of Jesus' life. Not proof, but good evidence. I thumbed through it quickly and found a chart he presents comparing the records of Jesus with those relaying other "facts" of ancient history.

"We believe that Julius Caesar was a real person and that what we know about him is mostly accurate history, right?"

"I suppose," Andrew conceded.

I turned the book toward him so he could make the comparison. "We have ten manuscripts of Caesar's *Gallic War,* and the oldest is dated AD 900, nearly one thousand years after the actual events. Livy's *Roman History*—we have twenty manuscripts dated from around AD 900. We accept our knowledge of ancient Greek history from writers like Herodotus. But we have only eight texts of his works, copied thirteen hundred years after his death. Compare these to existing copies of accounts of Jesus' life and teachings. We have nearly twenty-five thousand manuscripts of the New Testament, all nearly identical in content, dated within three hundred years of Jesus' time. Any objective historian would say we know more about Jesus than any other person in antiquity."

"Even so, he didn't write anything himself," replied Andrew. "These stories were spun by people with an agenda to protect their own power base. They aren't objective."

"Okay, the New Testament is biased. But the writers never claim objectivity. They are advocates, and say so. But these writers aren't out to protect their own reputation. They depict themselves in the stories as bumbling clods. It's Jesus, by contrast, who looks, well, perfect."

"Proving?"

"Nothing really. But if the New Testament is all spin, what is the agenda? What's the spin for? If these texts intend to bolster the authority of church leaders, they fail hands down. Front to back it casts light on Jesus alone. 'Heroes' like Peter and John come off as cowards and dimwits. Jesus alone is the agenda! Yet as you said, he's not the one writing. It's biased with no benefit to those being biased. Quite the opposite: The better they make Jesus look the more threat to their lives. After all, they're associating themselves with a convicted criminal and leader of a movement at war with a powerful establishment. Writing good words about Jesus brought these guys nothing but trouble. They must have believed their propaganda. At least it smells authentic."

I wished I had time to unfold for Andrew more detail, a story or two and some of Jesus' actual words. It's there we can catch glimpses of his true wonder. Had I found that chance, I might have shared this:

Like other first-century Jewish rabbis, Jesus moved from village to village telling stories. But he did more than teach. Jesus also challenged corruption in the government and announced that the long-promised era of justice had arrived. He even healed sick people with a touch of his hand. He called his revolution "the regime of God," and he claimed to be the tip of the spear bringing the change.

Three years after he launched his operation, Jesus made a journey from his home on the north shore of Lake Galilee to the capital city of Jerusalem, atop the Judean hills of southern Israel. He'd always worked on the move. Those who wanted to join his cause had to keep pace. Sometimes twenty or thirty followed. Sometimes thousands, but always he kept close to him the twelve young men he'd designated as his choice students. Their one responsibility was to stay close enough to their rabbi to "eat the dust" stirred up as he walked. On this particular trip Jesus and his band of men joined a stream of pilgrims on their way to celebrate the spring festival called Passover.

They arrived on the eighth day of the first month of the Jewish calendar, six days before Passover. Jesus paused on the road at the crest of the hill across the Kidron Valley from the city. Most of his fellow pilgrims knew his reputation. Many anticipated fireworks when he entered the gate. This festival would be the perfect moment for him to make his move. Curious watchers paused with him, and a hush fell as they waited to hear if he would make any pronouncement.

Jesus did not. He simply called two of his students and whispered something. Immediately, they set out toward the nearby village, and Jesus turned off the road, found a shaded spot, sat, and waited. A few from the crowd approached him. Some asked advice. Others sought a blessing on their children. A few begged him to command away a sickness.

Then his two minions returned leading a young donkey. When the crowd saw the animal they erupted. They knew what the donkey meant. Jesus had come to claim his place as King. The tradition, handed down centuries before, said Israel's True King would arrive on a donkey. The King of Peace would enter the City of Peace on a symbol of peace. Jesus asked for the donkey, tantamount to claiming the title

Messiah. The crowd chanted and danced. What a Passover this would be!

A few boys ran down the valley and up the hill toward the city, yelling as they flew along, "It's Jesus! He's coming—on a donkey." Word spread through the city like a firestorm. People flooded out the gate and up the road. Along the way some grabbed tree branches, and some found palms, which grew mostly down the steep ravines east of the city toward the Jordan River Valley and Jericho.

Palms had special significance. A century and a half before, a militia of Jewish revolutionaries led by Judas Maccabeus drove the Greek army out of Israel. Jews celebrate this improbable victory and the rededication of the temple with the feast of Hanukkah. The symbol of the Maccabean revolt was the palm branch; their battle cry: "Hosanna!" which means, "Lord, save us!"

The pilgrims and the mob from the city met and merged at the top of the hill as Jesus mounted the donkey and urged it forward. His young followers beamed. Their day had arrived. Everything he'd done had been but a prelude to this. This day was why they had left their families and endured so much to walk after him. Now Jesus would claim the crown; they would fight beside him and rule with him in his new government.

Thousands lined the road as the parade pressed forward. "Hosanna!" they shouted, waving palms and throwing their cloaks on the path before him.

"Well, clearly you believe Jesus was perfect," Andrew said.

"The writers thought so. And he did too, evidently. He said it and behaved like he believed it."

"How? How would someone claiming to be perfect behave?" Andrew pressed.

"For one thing, he treated social outcasts and women with dignity. And he ate meals with reputed criminals. In his culture, contact with outcasts would destroy a rabbi's status. Evidently, Jesus didn't fear catching their 'moral disease.' He felt secure in his own virtue, as if it couldn't be added to or subtracted from. And more than once he referred to himself as the true sacrificial lamb. Sacrificial lambs had to be flawless. He was arrogant, but maybe for good reason."

Not everyone in Jerusalem cheered Jesus' arrival. The political and religious center of Israel had its own resident rabbis— powerful, intellectual scholars who guarded their turf and looked askance at wannabes from Galilee. Many had sold out to the Romans, who governed the region. The Romans, of course, saw anyone who stirred populist and nationalist sentiment as a threat. Wedged between these conflicting forces, Israel balanced on a dangerous precipice. The last thing the power elite wanted was this Galilean do-gooder sparking the powder keg.

The power brokers too had heard rumors of Jesus. Without question he had accomplished astounding things: healing the sick, feeding thousands with a basket of food, even raising dead children back to life. But he had also said incendiary things to honorable people, shared meals with the riffraff, and deliberately fed a craving for liberation with talk of his "regime of God." No question: Jesus of Nazareth was a dangerous agitator.

What would Jesus do once he arrived in the city? Would he challenge the Jewish ruling council? Would he muster the Zealots and attack the Roman garrison? Would he storm Herod's palace? They knew from experience he could surprise them. Powerful people do not like surprises.

Months earlier Jesus had visited Jerusalem, and as usual a crowd gathered to hear his teaching. As he spoke, a group of religious teachers broke into his lesson, dragging behind them a woman they had evidently taken prisoner.

"We caught this woman in the very act of having sex with a man who is not her husband," one of them barked. Jesus studied them, perhaps wondering why they had not arrested her partner as well.

"What do we do with her?" they asked. "The Law says we should stone her. What do you say?" It was a setup, of course, similar to other traps they had sprung on Jesus. If he freed the woman, they could accuse him of contradicting Moses. If he condemned her, they would spin him to the masses as just another moral fanatic who really didn't care for people.

Jesus said nothing. Instead, he stooped and began to write in the dust. What, we are not told: a list of other sins and other sinners present? The Ten Commands of which the prohibition against adultery is but one? After an awkward silence, Jesus stood and looked into the eyes of his inquisitors. "All right," he answered, "but let the one who has never sinned throw the first stone."

They remained silent. Jesus waited. Then one by one, the men dropped the stones, turned and walked off in disgust, first the oldest among them, then the younger. The elders evidently had more to fear from public exposure of their personal morality.

Jesus stooped and wrote something more in the dust. Then he stood again and turned to the woman. "Where are your accusers?" he asked rhetorically. "Isn't anyone left to bring a charge against you, to condemn you to death?"

"No, Lord," she said.

"I don't condemn you either," he returned. "Go now, and be free, and stop throwing away God's gift of life as if it were dust in the wind."

Always a surprise!

"I've got to admire Jesus' audacity," Andrew said. "I remember that much from Sunday School."

"That audacity got him killed. And he didn't back down when he knew it was digging him in deep. He calmly claimed the right to forgive sin—to remove the consequences of bad choices. Taking up that authority meant claiming a divine right, a perfect divine right. The powerful around him labeled this blasphemy. It would be blasphemy, unless it was true."

"But Jesus made waves," Andrew objected. "Not everything he did or said resulted in peace. How can someone be perfect and cause a riot?" He sat up, sensing he'd hit on something solid.

"The negative reactions came from officials threatened by the freedom he offered to anyone willing to take it. Sure, those vested with power got angry. But their anger came from fear that he would expose their duplicity. Ugliness goes ballistic in the presence of goodness, and violence that tears down evil isn't necessarily evil itself."

"So, Jesus was a 'good' man." He smiled.

I shrugged. "It's just my call, but he seems to me to have been either perfectly good, or no good at all. He could not have been merely good. He was either what he said he was, or the greatest kook or con man ever."

"Your call," he echoed.

As the parade crossed the floor of the valley, Jesus pulled the donkey to a halt. Those closest pressed around him. Some moved to the side to catch a glimpse of his profile as he stared up toward the ancient city walls.

Tears swelled in his eyes, broke, and cut paths down his cheeks, mixing with the dust on his face. He spoke, to the city herself, as if no one else could hear him. "You are the City of Peace," he said, his voice trembling with passion. "That was God's intent. But now you will fall to dust. You have rejected your chance for peace." Then he spurred the donkey on toward the gate, and the crowd surged and shouted again.

At the entrance of the city Jesus dismounted. Roman troops on high alert watched from their posts on the top of the wall. The crowds chanted. Excitement. Anxiety. Tension swept into the city ahead of him. Something would soon break.

Jesus walked through the gate and headed straight toward the temple. His twelve followed on his heels. Every moment now, every word, action, and response would be pregnant with significance. They wouldn't miss a thing.

Jesus entered the courtyard of the temple, paused, and clenched his fists. As always, merchants had set up tables there in anticipation of arriving pilgrim customers. The week before Passover offered a retail bonanza. Temple tradesmen held a monopoly sanctioned by the ruling council, allowing them to charge inflated prices for "approved" livestock fit for sacrifice. Jesus exploded in a rage. How dare these fiends profit off people's desire to worship God! He grabbed a rope lying on the ground, quickly braided it into a whip, and charged down the line, overturning tables and driving out animals and their handlers.

"This is a sacred place of prayer and you have turned it into a hideout for hoodlums," he bellowed.

Surprise!

Then to the bewilderment of everyone in the city, Jesus turned and walked through the flotsam and jetsam in his wake and headed out of the city. No march on Herod's palace; no storming the headquarters of Pilate, the Roman governor; just this single show of fury and force against the artisans of holy commerce. This after such pent-up anticipation? Jesus retraced his steps across the Kidron Valley and headed toward the village of Bethany. His twelve confused followers tagged behind, mumbling to each other and trying to clear their throats of the dust he stirred.

Each day leading up to Passover, Jesus reentered the gates of Jerusalem, though now without any fanfare or parade. The city seemed perplexed. Would he make a move? He taught in the temple, then before sunset returned to Bethany. His advocates grew impatient, and ordinary citizens grew disillusioned. The political leaders felt the tide of opinion turning against him and began pushing the momentum further. Secretly they plotted a final solution. In private, Jesus' twelve followers asked him to explain his intentions. He answered with his typical cryptic lines and parables. What could it mean? What would happen?

On Thursday morning, just hours before Passover, the Jewish feast recounting the miraculous escape from Egyptian slavery, Jesus remained in Bethany and sent Peter and John into the city to find a room and prepare the meal his band would share together that evening.

At sundown, after the streets had emptied and most citizens and pilgrims were feasting in homes or inns, Jesus and his men made their way through the dusty, dung-littered alleys, down to the southwest section of Jerusalem.

The mood felt surreal as they climbed the stairs to the secluded room Peter and John had secured. Once more they all wondered, "What would Jesus do next?" His followers sensed his work had come to some climax. He'd said so, though no one understood the hints about dying and returning to life. What about the triumphant march five days prior? Why had he not mustered an army?

Just like the crowds, Jesus' closest followers still cast him in the popular depiction of Messiah. He would become king, of course, and they would serve in his government: Nathaniel as secretary of defense, perhaps; Andrew as chief of staff; and Judas, secretary of the treasury.

As the suspense and anticipation around him mounted in the preceding month, the twelve had begun jockeying for position. They anticipated a coup and a revolution. They had each watched and waited for chances to prove themselves worthy of his trust. Now here they were, eating the sacred feast of Passover in a secret hideaway. Why? What did it mean? What did *he* mean?

They stepped through the door and into an awkward moment. For a few breaths each man hung his head and avoided eye contact. Someone cleared his throat again. No one moved. Peter and John, the hosts of the evening, stepped out of the shadows. They too sensed the tension. They had finalized meal preparations of roasted lamb, bitter greens, bread, wine, and fruit, but now everyone stood waiting for someone else to do something, the something that had to be done.

Normally, it fell to the servant of each household to wash the feet of guests. Evidently this rented room had not come with an assigned servant. In lieu of a servant, tradition prescribed that the one with the least clout in the household should do the deed. But after spending a week maneuvering for power positions in the transition team, no one wanted to admit to the "least" slot in the pecking order. They all stood, waiting for someone else to buckle.

Clean feet held more than ritualistic significance. They mattered for practical reasons as well. In that culture diners took their meals leaning on pillows around a knee-high table, reclining on one elbow, extending their feet beside them, often near their neighbor's face. After walking dusty and littered roads in open sandals, they came to dinner with filthy feet.

Something had to give. Finally, one by one the young men tossed aside their cloaks, turned, and found their places around the table. Evidently they would simply overlook the matter and get on with the meal.

Rabbis teach not merely with words, but with actions. Jesus had said on several occasions, "The first will be last; the last will be first." And "If you want to be great in my regime, you must be the servant of everyone else." Now he would demonstrate what this meant.

At some point in the middle of the sacred meal Jesus surprised them again. He stood and walked toward the door. As they watched him, he took off his outer robe and wrapped a towel around his waist, took up the wash basin of water, and came back toward the table. One by one he moved around the circle, washing dust from the feet of the young men.

They blushed in shame. When Jesus came to Peter, he gave voice to his embarrassment. "I can't let you do this . . ." he objected. "Unless you let me serve you," Jesus responded, "we can have no relationship at all. These are the terms."

Good God! we want to say back to him. *Who do you think you are?* Who? indeed. There is something terrible and frightening about his audacity. Jesus' simple confidence terrorizes our sensibilities. People, especially powerful people, have never stomached this well. He holds no qualms about declaring his own virtue, a virtue he expresses—to no benefit of his own—by washing the dust from the feet of his followers, healing and touching a leper whose physical and social contamination became his own, announcing forgiveness to an adulterous woman, and finally by offering himself as a sacrificial lamb.

I wondered what else I could say to Andrew. How hard could I press my perspective without pressing him? I wanted to ask him straight up. This something we see in Jesus, this perfect, unabashed and unflinching kindness, could it be the essence of love? What if Jesus had—what if he was— perfect love? We recognize pure love when we see it because it startles the familiar laws of survival that drive our world. Jesus is out of place!

This perfect love always startles us. Charles Dickens' novel *A Tale of Two Cities* opens and closes with two of the most famous lines in literature. "It was the best of times, it

was the worst of times . . ." Dickens writes in the first line.
He closes, "It is a far, far better thing that I do, than I have
ever done; it is a far, far better rest that I go to than I have
ever known." In between, Dickens weaves a solemn, lofty
narrative depicting the inevitable decay of human evil and
surprising innocent triumph of heavenly goodness in the
form of love.

Set against the horrors of the French revolution, this
novel tells the tale of Charles Darnay and Sydney Carton,
two men who look alike yet bear starkly different personalities. Darnay, a French aristocrat, and Carton, a wasted and
cynical English lawyer, each fall in love with Lucie Manette.
When Darnay is condemned to the guillotine, Carton, who
recognizes that Lucie would be far more fulfilled with Darnay than with him, arranges to secretly take Darnay's place
in the execution.

Dickens depicts in Carton goodness that makes no natural sense. His actions serve no evolutionary genetic motive.
He dies to save another—love in its highest, most heavenly
form. "Greater love has no one than this," Jesus told his
friends soon after he had wiped the last of the dust from
their calloused feet, "that he lay down his life for a friend."
Carton, who seems anything but good throughout the
novel, rises in the end to perfect goodness by stooping to
serve in the lowest of ways. We see this and instantly recognize the parallel: He's like Jesus! Readers respond to Carton
because we understand deeply that he discovers the essence
of life—to live, and die if need be, for another, though the
sacrifice reaches beyond our own self-interest.

In his book *The Four Loves*, C. S. Lewis talks about
the different human experiences we attempt to pack into
the English word *love*. The Greeks, says Lewis, had four

different words for the states of love we attempt to cover with one. *Eros* is erotic, or sexual passion. We call this "falling in love." *Phileo* is camaraderie and friendship, the way we endear a friend. *Storge* is affection for familiar things— warm comfort for and from an old pair of shoes or a loyal dog. *Agape*, Lewis claims, trumps them all as selfless sacrifice. The initial three loves grow out of instinct, and in some ways serve our own interests. They are natural and therefore amoral. Only the last love, agape, stands above our instincts. It reveals and preserves the genetic code of God's heart written within us, the instinct of divinity. Apart from God's own gift of himself, we have no capacity to find agape or to practice it. We might recognize it when we see it, in Carton for instance, but left to our own devices we can never generate it. We're far too bound up in ourselves.

Could this agape—seeking another's best interest at the expense of our own—describe the essence of the "perfect goodness" we see in Jesus? The evidence might indicate this—that Jesus lived and loved at a superhuman level. Seeing him at work, hearing his words, sensing his piercing, alert consciousness we might just catch a faint hint of some sweet memory emanating from back beyond our childhood. In Jesus we might witness perfection as we know it should have been all along and should be forevermore. Could such perfection create consequences as perfectly good? Why not?

Why not "perfect" Karma?

"So if Karma is one of the laws of the universe," I said, thinking out loud, "and Karma dictates that everyone bear responsibility for what they cause, and if that dooms us because we all cause more trouble than we're worth and can never pay

our debts, and if Jesus not only does good, but truly IS good, and if his goodness is so complete that he has to share it with others, could Jesus be a kind of cosmic exemption?" I said this groping for an idea I knew I didn't understand.

"You mean, like a wormhole connecting different parts of reality?" Andrew offered.

"A wormhole?" Not something I expected to hear, first because Andrew seemed to be adding to my point, not countering it, and second because I didn't easily marry fuzzy theories from astrophysics with my theology. I shrugged. "Yeah, maybe so."

"A shortcut or short circuit through time and space . . . an interesting way to explain what you're trying to say." Andrew seemed to be running ahead of me and giving me credit for more creative brilliance than I deserved.

"Say more," I asked.

Andrew sat back. "After Einstein figured out general relativity, other theorists realized there could be portals or bridges that connect distant regions of time-space. Today they call these wormholes. If we could ever move through a wormhole we might travel faster than light, and maybe even travel back and forward in time. Wild stuff, and something Einstein himself said would break the laws of nature."

"So one law seems to break another, leaving open the chance that there might be shortcuts from one part of reality to another," I offered.

Andrew shrugged. "Maybe."

"Then . . ." I reached for the link. "Karma is bad news. Jesus beat Karma at its own game and earned the right to use it against itself. His pure goodness allowed him to swap Karma with the rest of us, who, as we've seen, are anything but good. Jesus' perfect life makes . . . a wormhole."

"Karma doesn't allow cheating. That's the whole point. We reap what we sow," Andrew reminded me. "But then, the universe doesn't allow anything faster than light either. But then it does, with wormholes. Remember the principle in chemistry, 'Like dissolves like'?"

"Yeah," I said, only half honest.

"Polar solvents like water dissolve polar solutes like salt. Oil is nonpolar, so water and oil not only don't mix, they don't dissolve together. But like dissolves like, polar dissolves polar, so water dissolves salt."

"So can Karma dissolve Karma? Wouldn't perfect Karma dissolve Karma perfectly? We can't break the rules, but a perfect person can neutralize them. Only a person with perfect Karma can take up the imperfect Karma of everyone and everything else and 'dissolve' it into himself. And like that, he 'shortcuts' reality."

Andrew seemed to have joined me in this dizzying speculation. "I think Buddhists have a caveat to Karma called transfer of merit."

"Every religion admits the idea in some form. Maybe Jesus takes the theory and makes it reality, actually lives it out. What if he takes his real, historical goodness and gives it away to anyone who asks, and then in reverse takes all our blight into himself?"

"The garbage has to go somewhere," Andrew added. Then he thought a moment. "And that would be massively stupid."

"Yes, except that Jesus is good, and goodness is love, selfless love."

Andrew considered the implications.

"One of Jesus' first followers wrote of it this way," I said. "And perhaps you remember these lines from your childhood: 'For God so loved the world that he gave his one and only Son, that whoever believes in him shall not perish but have eternal life.' "

"It just seems foolish. What's in it for him?" Andrew said pensively.

"You are. I am. Evidently, we're all he really wants out of life."

CHRIST SUBMERGED

"You're making Karma out to be what you usually call sin," Andrew said.

"That's fair," I answered. "Christians say sin is much more than all the things we do wrong. It's the cumulated garbage of all human generations piled up into my DNA. Karma and sin: the same bad news."

"So why did Jesus die?" Andrew circled back to his core question.

"The short answer: His heart stopped," I said.

Andrew blew air through his teeth in mock disgust. "Touché."

"Okay, seriously, Jesus died because he threatened powerful people. They couldn't frighten him; that frightened them. So they killed him. A lot of revolutionaries meet this fate. Athens couldn't tolerate Socrates. Radical Hindus couldn't tolerate Gandhi. Segregationists couldn't tolerate Martin Luther King—"

Andrew cut in. "That's not what I meant. His supporters make Jesus out to be more than a martyr—as if his death accomplished something in itself."

"Maybe it did. Many people think so. They believe Jesus' death took spiritual toxins out of the world and released goodness back. This is why people say Jesus saves."

The line didn't faze him. Andrew waited for more.

I once told a joke during one of my talks: Satan claimed he could write better computer programs than Jesus. Jesus disputed this. So they decided to settle the matter with a contest judged by God.

Jesus and Satan sat at their respective computers. God gave the word and each began typing furiously. Lines of code began streaming across their screens. Hours passed and still they pounded away on their keyboards.

Then, just seconds before the end of the competition, a thunderstorm rolled over and a bolt of lightning took out the electricity. A moment later the power returned as God declared an end to the contest.

God asked Satan to unveil his work. Satan shook with frustration, pulled the hair from his goatee, and cursed. "I have nothing," he fumed. "I lost it all when the power went out."

"Very well, then," God replied. "Let's see if Jesus fared any better."

Jesus serenely entered a command. Instantly his screen came to life with a display that could only be described as divinely ingenious. Voices of an angelic choir poured from the speakers as a time-lapsed version of the history of the universe unfolded in ninety seconds.

"Very impressive," said God.

Satan's face went red with fury. "B-b-but how?" he stuttered. "I lost everything. How did he do it?"

God smiled. "Jesus saves."

Andrew had heard this line or seen it painted on sandwich boards draped over the shoulders of barking street preachers. He'd read it on bathroom stalls like everyone else. It's a cliché, which is why we laugh—or groan—at the pun.

But what does it mean? Looking at it through Andrew's eyes, I too had to wonder.

Jesus saves the whales?

Jesus saves his tip money in a glass jar?

Jesus drives a hybrid to save gas?

Commonly used English words have an average of twenty-six meanings each. So Jesus saves . . . what?

Clearly Jesus lived differently from the rest of us. He walked out onto the ledge of the edge of the world and said and did things there that defy human experience. Not many have put breath back into the bodies of dead children and then gone on with their day as if nothing extraordinary had happened. What sane person boasts moral perfection? Jesus defied description. His life was either too good to be true or too good not to be true.

Yet Jesus claimed—and those who knew him best agreed—that the pivotal point of his existence came at his sudden execution. His death mattered more than his extraordinary life. What happened to Jesus on a Roman cross in AD 33 still scandalizes the imagination.

"Did you ever see Mel Gibson's The Passion of the Christ? I asked.

"Grotesque," Andrew answered.

"Gibson actually downplayed the cruelty." I went on to give a layman's explanation of the torture, as I had heard it explained.

The Roman penal system devised the vilest instrument of cruel and unusual punishment in the history of human-kind: crucifixion. They crucified criminals by the thou-sands as punishment and a deterrent against insurgency. The pain inflicted proved so monstrous it spawned a new word: *excruciating.* It means "from the cross."

Gibson etches just part of the picture in blood and gore. First, soldiers bound their victim to a post and flogged him with thirty-nine lashes from a whip of nine leather strands, each with a strip of jagged steel tied to the tip. The lash-ing tore through the skin and into the muscle. Eusebius, a third-century historian, described the torture this way: "The sufferer's veins were laid bare, and the very muscles, sinews, and bowels of the victim were exposed."

The executioners then spread the prisoner's arms across a rough wooden beam and drove nine-inch tapered spikes through the median nerve in each wrist. The wracking pain would be comparable to taking a vise grip and grabbing hold of the nerve we call the funny bone and crushing it. Next, they suspended the beam and attached it to a perpen-dicular post ten feet above the ground. A third spike drilled the prisoner's feet to the post.

Death came slowly, by suffocation more than from blood loss. To breathe, the prisoner had to push up against the spike in his feet, pull out against the spikes through his wrists, and arch his back to free his diaphragm. The war between the instinct to breathe and the dread of the nause-ating pulses of pain could last for hours, even days.

Jesus suffered. But eye witnesses reported that he did speak several times during the ordeal. They recorded his words, which suggest Jesus believed his torment served some mysterious, universal purpose.

At one point Jesus addressed God. "Father, forgive those who have done this to me. They don't understand what they are doing." He believed the injustice as well as the outcome of this crime remained hidden from his enemies. Instead of calling for revenge, he asked God to cover their guilt.

He spoke to one of the murderers hanging beside him and assured him, "Today you will come with me to a safe and splendid place." This horror might end his earthly existence, but good would triumph in the end, for him and for those who sided with him.

He also addressed his mother and John, his closest friend. "John, please care for her as you would your own mother."

Then, at his darkest point of despair, he cried, "My God, my God, why have you deserted me to this?" God, whom he called Father, had remained an intimate presence all his life. Now, suddenly, had his Father turned away? Or had something about this experience blocked Jesus' ability to detect the Father's presence? The prospect terrified Jesus.

Finally, as death enveloped him, he shouted out, "It is finished! Father, I give you back the life you've given me." He said this; then he died. What was finished? A mission? What mission?

As the full weight of Jesus' limp body collapsed against the wounds in his wrists and feet, bizarre events began to unfold. Though four hours of daylight remained, the sky turned black. A thunderstorm exploded over the hills of Jerusalem, hurling down lightning bolts, rain, and hail. An earthquake jarred the city. Had the earth itself gone into seizure with spasms of grief? In the Jewish temple in Jerusalem, the curtain that walled off the most sacred chamber from the rest of the building ripped in two, top to bottom. What? Why? Other good people had been wrongly executed. Why all this at the moment? Why for Jesus?

Jesus died on a Friday afternoon. The Jewish Sabbath began at sunset, so officials wanted to remove the body quickly. Sympathizers took Jesus' body to the tomb of a wealthy friend. A massive stone closed off the entrance, and Pilate, the Roman governor of Judea, who had ordered the crucifixion, marked it off-limits with his own official seal. Then he posted guards.

Nothing changed Friday night through Saturday and Saturday night.

But before sunrise on Sunday something inexplicable occurred. Something, or someone, rolled away the stone—an event so startling that the soldiers on guard fled in terror. Later, when some of Jesus' followers came to the tomb to wrap his corpse in spices, they found the body gone. Vanished. Later that day they began spreading the story that they had seen Jesus alive and had even talked with him.

What actually happened? The riddle has never been solved to everyone's satisfaction. Had Jesus survived the ordeal and somehow set himself free? How likely is that? Victims didn't survive crucifixion; certainly not with enough strength to push aside a monstrous stone and overpower armed soldiers.

Had his friends stolen the body? That seems psychologically improbable. Where had they found the courage to do that when two days before they had all deserted him to save their own skins? And if they did conspire, why would they all later embrace martyrdom? To protect a secret? Surely someone would have talked.

Circumstantial evidence suggests some sort of wonder. In the weeks and months immediately following, the circle of those who called themselves *believers* exploded from 120 to close to ten thousand. Stories of powerful personal transformations fueled this expansion. Advocates claimed that Jesus had died and then come back to life and in that process had tilted the spiritual axis of the planet; that his death had thwarted evil and his new life had released creative power into the world.

People claimed to have experienced this phenomenon personally. They said that acknowledging belief in Jesus purged them of guilt for their past sins. By identifying with Jesus, they said they had "died" with him and had buried the residue of their past, and that as he came back to life, they too had found a chance to begin again.

As stories of this experience multiplied, the instrument of Jesus' execution—the Roman cross—became a symbol of miraculous personal renewal. No one today wears a silver locket depicting an electric chair, but millions wear a cross as a statement of faith and identification with the power of this mysteriously persistent story.

Andrew listened to me ramble, and finally cut in: "A lot of cultures perpetuate myths of a god who dies and comes back to life. Christians just read this pattern backward and apply it to Jesus."

"Okay," I admitted. "But what if Jesus is real history?"

"How can that be?"

"The Egyptians had Osiris. The Norse had Odin. The Greeks had Adonis. In their myths, these gods die and come back to life. But people in those cultures didn't actually believe the gods lived inside their world as part of their history. The difference with Jesus is that he lived out this pattern in real time and in a real place. What if the old myths were just a kind of premonition, something planted to prepare us for the real thing? What if Jesus' life and death were that real thing?"

"Too weird," he said.

"Well, like I said before, there are more accounts of Jesus' life and death than there are accounts of the life and death of Julius Caesar. Yet we consider Caesar's story irrefutable history. What if the Jesus story is the old myths come to life?"

Andrew shook his head, and then looked away. I wanted to read his thoughts, but a fog bank seemed to separate us. Perhaps he was mulling over the questions.

Had Jesus lived a perfect life and died an unjust death?

Strange events did occur the day he died and in the days following. Could the claims of mysterious power emanating from his death have any credibility?

Did Jesus choose to absorb evil and its consequences in his death?

Did his trip through the underbelly of existence manage to kill evil itself?

Could he have borne away "Karma" and buried it somewhere in the back lot of the cosmos, then returned to this life free and able to grant that freedom to all who asked for it?

Jesus saves?

Ancient Jews anticipated the possibility of total and complete salvation. Every autumn Jews celebrated Yom Kippur, the Day of Atonement. Many still do. Like many religious ceremonies, Yom Kippur originally involved the slaughter of animals. Ancient people believed that life resides in the blood. By ritually killing animals, they believed they could exchange the animal's life for the debt they incurred by their own moral failures.

On Yom Kippur, Jewish priests sacrificed one goat and used its blood to cleanse from sin. They then imposed a very different destiny on a second goat. Instead of killing it, the lead priest placed his hands on the creature's head and began to recite—in detail—all the failures of the entire nation in the previous year. Imagine a public reading of the "naughty" ledger of Santa's list.

This confession, they believed, transferred their corporate guilt onto the goat—their scapegoat. Once they completed the ritual, they drove the poor beast into the desert, symbolically bearing their load of shame and blame into desolate places.

Could it be that Jesus took up both roles—the sacrificed life that paid for the full consequence of sin and the scapegoat that carried the sin far away to be forgotten?

"So Jesus' death makes evil and the effects of evil magically disappear?" asked Andrew skeptically. "Things don't just disappear. I think you said that. They have to go somewhere, right? Explain this."

"I can't. But a lot of usable things have no explanation. Aspirin prevents heart attacks and lowers fever, but experts can't say why, exactly. They only know it works."

"Maybe. But some people might say that such a horrible death proves that Jesus had terrible Karma, that he must have done something atrocious to warrant that kind of misery."

"Mmm. I'll have to think about that," I said, somewhat taken aback. "But remember, death didn't happen to Jesus. He didn't run from it. He actually walked into it. And his followers reported that he told them ahead of time what was going to happen and how. It was as though he chose to embrace it. I can see how what you're saying would apply if Jesus had been a victim. But he made the choice to die."

"Sounds like a madman."

"That or someone madly in love with the world doing the only thing that could fix what's wrong with it."

I knew full well that I couldn't satisfy Andrew's curiosity for a definitive answer. People a whole lot smarter than me have tried to explain how Jesus' death "works," and how his actions paid the debt incurred by our sins and neutralized the repercussions. Philosophers call these ideas "theories of atonement." Several versions exist, but they fall into three basic categories. I briefly described each idea.

Origen, an Egyptian bishop in the second century, understood Jesus' crucifixion as the ultimate tactic of war against evil, and specifically against the devil, whom he believed to be a literal being. Because of sin, Origen said, humans owe Satan a debt only death can pay. So when a perfect human—Jesus—died, he covered that debt in full by conquering the basis of the debt itself. This broke Satan's power.

In Peter Benchley's book and the 1975 film *Jaws*, the great white shark that terrorizes a New England beach community is hunted down and destroyed by Police Chief Martin Brody, the grizzled fisherman Captain Quint, and a shark scientist, Matt Hooper. At the climax, Quint is killed by the shark, but Brody hurls one of Hooper's oxygen tanks into the beast's gaping mouth. He then detonates that tank with a well-aimed rifle shot. The creature explodes because it has devoured the very weapon of its destruction. Origen might say that Jesus defeated Satan by tricking him into swallowing death itself. We might call it the "Jaws theory" of atonement with Jesus tricking his adversary into swallowing death and thereby conquering death itself.

A second theory came from Peter Abelard, who defined Jesus' atonement in a simpler and more down-to-earth way. Abelard, born in France in 1079, said that Jesus' power was authority-by-example. Jesus' gentle response to his unjust execution inspires us to love in the face of evil. When we love, we neutralize the evil in the world. Anyone who follows Jesus' example in essence becomes "Jesus" in the world and joins him in undercutting the power of wickedness.

Many accounts in history can demonstrate this principle, but the following story from World War II relays it as clearly as any.

One day in 1941, during roll call at the Nazi extermination camp at Auschwitz, Colonel Fritsch, the camp commandant, stopped in front of a prisoner named Francis Gajowniczek. He looked at the young man and called out his number: 5659. It was Gajowniczek's death sentence.

The day before, a prisoner had escaped. The Nazis had warned the inmates that for every escaped prisoner ten would starve to death. After forcing the prisoners to stand in formation all day in the hot sun, Fritsch walked through their columns, randomly stopping and calling out the numbers of ten men.

When he read Gajowniczek's number, the poor man broke down. He said later that his thoughts flew to his wife and their two children. He cried aloud, saying how sorry he was for his family.

Several seconds passed. Then number 16670 broke ranks. His head was slightly bent as he came to attention and identified himself in front of the commandant. They spoke in German, and those nearby heard the conversation.

"What does this Polish pig want?" asked Fritsch. The man, Maximilian Kolbe, replied, "I am a Catholic priest and I am old; I would like to take this man's place. He has a wife and children."

Stupefied, the commandant looked around and said simply, "Here's a crazy priest." But for some reason he then added, "All right."

And that struck the deal. Two weeks later, Maximilian Kolbe died for Francis Gajowniczek. The act did not in itself defeat the Nazis or satisfy the insane perversion of Fritsch's thirst for blood. But Kolbe's act of love bolstered the courage of the prisoners and served as a living example of personal honor that stands stronger than institutional barbarity. Simple love trumped the enemy's ultimate weapon—the fear of death.

Was Jesus a Kolbe-like martyr who broke the fear of evil with fearless love? Many people today have taken up Abelard's theory as a viable interpretation of Jesus' life and death and suggest that Kolbe was like Jesus in the world.

There's a third interpretation. It came from Anselm of Canterbury, who lived just one generation before Abelard. Anselm explained the power of the cross in a logical but somewhat troubling way. He argued that Jesus' death paid man's debt to God himself. God demanded perfect obedience, and our failures forced God to level justice upon our heads. It could not be avoided. Anselm said that Jesus stepped between us and God's hand of punishment. This allowed God to vent his wrath and keep the legal requirement of justice without destroying all humanity.

One incomplete picture of Anselm's idea is the musical *West Side Story*, Shakespeare's *Romeo and Juliet* recast in New York City in the 1950s. The two feuding families are replaced by brawling street gangs—the white immigrant Jets and the Puerto Rican immigrant Sharks. Tony, a Jet, meets and falls in love with Maria, the sister of Bernardo, the leader of the Sharks. Their stars cross and their tragedy unfolds. With opposition from both sides, the lovers meet secretly and their passion and commitment grow. As the gangs plot one last battle, Tony steps in to stop the feud and is shot by Chino, who was jealous for Maria's love. Tony dies in Maria's arms. She then grabs Chino's gun and in terrible grief denounces the stupid hatred that has caused the strife. As Maria collapses in sorrow, the two gangs surround her, now united in their common grief. Tragically, the wrath of each side was satisfied as Tony stepped in to absorb at a terrible cost the brunt of the injustice.

But then, every atonement explanation has its critics. To Origen, we can ask, "Why does God have to pay a ransom to the devil? Doesn't this diminish God's power to that of a glorified bail bond dealer?"

To Abelard: "A kind heart is all well and good, but what ultimate good is without the power to stop evil itself? Besides, if Jesus simply offers an example for us to follow, who of us loves as perfectly as Jesus? At the end of the day, evil remains and justice remains unsatisfied."

Anselm makes us cringe. "What a picture of God! The Almighty comes off looking like a bloodthirsty sadist or vengeful street gang member who practices child abuse on his own son just to pacify his own anger issues."

"Bottom line," I said to Andrew, "we don't know how Jesus takes bad things out of the world and releases good things in their place. But people who have experienced him doing it swear that it happens."

"Your wormhole! Maybe Jesus is quantum." Andrew chuckled. "Light is a wave and a particle. Logically it can't be both, but when they look for it as a wave, it is a wave. When they measure it as a particle, it's a particle. You get the reality you expect."

"That makes my head spin," I admitted.

"So?" Andrew waited for me to connect the dots. He obviously wasn't going to.

"So maybe atonement theories are quantum," I said tentatively.

Andrew shrugged as if this was obvious. I wondered suddenly who was teaching whom.

"Sure," I said. "Maybe Jesus' death becomes whatever we expect it to be, or whatever we need him to be. He's a warrior, he's an example, he's an advocate who intercedes for us, and he's all these things all at once. Maybe the power of each role gets activated once we decide based on our own need and act in faith for one or the other."

"Quantum Jesus—the cosmic wormhole. That's pretty crazy," Andrew mused. But he seemed quite serious.

"Then again, maybe there's a fourth way to say it. Maybe different people and cultures need the cross of Jesus to be different things for them. Maybe in our day the answer is

Karma." I said this and the ideas in our entire conversation seemed to coalesce within me.

"Could be," he answered casually. And for the fourth or fifth time in our discussion I sensed him growing distant and aloof, as if he'd suddenly determined not to take any of this personally.

"Our Karma ends up unmanageable, right?" I said again. "Maybe in our day, the atonement of Jesus has become the solution to Karma's doom. Maybe it's as simple as 'Jesus is the answer; what's the question?' And the question for us is, 'What can I do with my Karma?' "

"Since things don't disappear, they're exchanged . . ." Andrew muttered.

"Maybe that's what was happening when the world shook and went as black as night when he died. But the *how* doesn't matter. *Somehow* says enough," I said. "But the cost on his part, however it worked, was unimaginable."

"Maybe," said Andrew. He looked tired.

I certainly was. I searched for a new handle or a second wind.

I first watched the short film *Most* (the word in Czech means "the bridge") on my computer over a lunch hour. It destroyed the rest of my day and changed how I understood God. I wished I had it for Andrew in place of my tired words.

Most was shot in the Czech Republic and Poland by producer/writer William Zabka and producer/director Bobby Garabedian. In 2004, the film was nominated for an Oscar in the Short Film (Live Action) category.

The film tells the story of the tender relationship between a father and his son on the fateful day the father, a railroad bridge operator, decides to take his son to work with him.

As a crowded train speeds ahead of schedule toward the open drawbridge, the father rushes to head off the railroad disaster. Aware of the crisis, the son himself crawls into the engine well to try to move the gears.

Finally, the father must make the most painful choice imaginable. He flips the switch and lowers the bridge to save the train, crushing his only son in the process.

Most depicts a vision of atonement that goes beyond a battle against evil, an example to follow, and a way to mediate vengeance. It depicts salvation as an act of love that carries with it an incalculable cost. Just as when God chose to "crush" his only son, the choice came not from anger but pain-laden love.

There's a cost to saving the world from its Karma. The garbage has to go somewhere. Someone has to pay the bill.

I knew from personal experience what I was saying.

My wife, Jill, and I recently celebrated our twenty-fifth wedding anniversary. Yet we almost crashed and burned five years ago when we diagnosed a cancer in our relationship. Our marriage survived only because of the mystery of the cross.

The seed of the sickness began ten years ago, when I began a PhD program at Regent University. When I first took the idea to Jill, she seemed cautious. We had four small children and not much money, and to complete this program I would have to maintain my full-time job. Not a great prospect for a "real" life.

Still, I persisted, and I can be convincing. I eventually wore her down and won her concession, her permission, but not her blessing. Inside she resented it.

I studied hard for four years. *In the long run this will be good for the family,* I told myself. It would open doors. But the cost was high. Jill went on with the business of raising our children. And for all intents and purposes, she went on alone. My work and my studies tapped my best time and best energy. In those years, I admit, I gave little to Jill or the children.

In the months after I completed my studies, I began to re-engage with my family. But I found a wall separating us. One day Jill and I went for a walk in the woods behind our house. Jill aired her pain and anger, and she warned me that if we didn't get help she could no longer live with me.

I hadn't known until that moment the gravity of our crisis. I agreed to go with her to see a counselor named Ron Keller. Our sessions with Ron began a process that changed our lives.

Ron helped us identify the origin of our rift—my decision to press Jill to agree to the doctoral studies. We knew this was the core, because when we hit that subject, Jill's deep hurt began to pour out. So did my guilt.

Those first sessions brought clarity but no relief. We learned the name of the cancer destroying us. But diagnosis was not the same as treatment or cure. The matter came to a head on a Wednesday afternoon after an hour with Ron. We had clarity in our crisis: I needed pardon, Jill needed to extend pardon. But we had nowhere to dump the acidic toxins eating holes in our souls.

We decided that day to attend a weekend marriage seminar called *Sanctus*—the Latin word for sacred—led by a therapist named Wilfred Sager. Dr. Sager believes that marriage can move us into what the ancient Celts call a "thin place"—a world between the physical and spiritual worlds. It can open a doorway that is down-to-earth and ordinary yet holy and mysteriously transcendent.

We attended the conference reluctantly. The barrier between us was so stark we didn't even want to sit together. But out of sheer stubbornness we decided to walk along the steppingstones Wilfred outlined.

Then on Saturday morning the dam broke. Wilfred talked about forgiveness, about identifying the pain from hurts we had received and the guilt from hurts we had caused. He said that identifying hurt and guilt didn't fix them. They had to go somewhere, away from our lives. We might express ourselves and vent our anger and cry out in regret, but unless the poisonous root is removed, nothing really changes. Getting it out, he said, is beyond our own ability. That takes a miracle, a hand from outside.

Then Wilfred walked through the room, handing each couple a crucifix—a wooden cross with an image of a disfigured Jesus on it.

The crucifix is common in ancient expressions of the Christian faith. Jill and I grew up in Protestant churches that shunned this image. But Wilfred had an agenda. He asked us as a couple to hold the crucifix in our hands. Jill and I reluctantly followed his guidance. We would never have held hands otherwise, but with the crucifix between us, we together grasped it tightly. Our hands and fingers met around the cold metal emaciated figure. We held on.

Then Wilfred prayed. He asked God to come now and flush out our pain and our guilt. He asked God to pour all the sewage into Jesus, represented by the image on that crucifix. Then he waited. We waited.

Suddenly it happened. Words escape me now. I can only describe the outcome. As we sat there clutching the cross, we both began to weep. Our shoulders heaved and hot tears poured down our faces. It was as if the plugs of our souls were pulled, and the stench of betrayal flowed out. Our hands grew hot and damp as the poison emanated from our grasp. It went somewhere. The poison went into the poor, crushed man on the cross.

We felt ourselves lifted out of time and across the planet, back to a real moment. We came to the foot of that ancient instrument of execution on a hill outside the city of Jerusalem. And though we live two thousand years and thousands of miles removed, it all became our moment. Jesus bore our Karma, the vile consequences of hurting and being hurt in ways neither of us could repair. He took it and bore the "divorce" in our place.

There as we sat together, now suddenly truly together, we seemed to hear simultaneously Jesus' words on the cross, "My God, my God, why have you deserted me to this?" That was our "divorce"—divorcing Jesus from God. Our crisis leaped across time and transferred from us to Jesus. In its place—out of him—poured love and grace and tender affection.

In an instant we were healed and intimate again. All pain and guilt washed away. That night we celebrated the miracle. And still today, though the chasm remains part of our story, it is a distant part, kept alive only when we recall what happened as a way of expressing our gratitude to Jesus and sharing our hope with others who have their own impossible chasms to cross. We still have our struggles, but now we know where to go with them.

Miracles do happen. They happen because on the cross our Karma became his, and his became ours.

"Did you ever see Piss Christ?" I asked.

The question broke through Andrew's tiredness. "Heard of it," he said. "It made Jesse Helms mad."

Indeed. *Piss Christ*, the controversial photograph by American photographer Andres Serrano, depicts a plastic crucifix submerged in a glass of the author's urine. In 1989, the work earned Serrano a $15,000 award from the government-funded National Endowment for the Arts. Helms and other lawmakers went ballistic, calling the NEA's grant governmental support for a religious statement against God.

"Jesus never testified in those congressional hearings," I told Andrew. "He never defended himself. No lightning fell. Serrano's hands didn't break out with leprosy. The urine did not turn to wine. As far as I can tell, God sat silently and bore the defamation."

"That's one way to look at it," Andrew responded.

I kept on my point. "I remember an interview that Bill Moyers did with Wendy Beckett, a Catholic nun—that art critic with a television series of her own. Have you seen her? She begged to differ with the popular sentiment that Serrano's work blasphemes Jesus. A nun! She said, 'This is what we are doing to Christ.' I used to imagine God up there poised to lower the boom, ticked off at my defiance."

"Me too," Andrew agreed.

"But what if Serrano had it right?" I continued. "Could God be the victim, not the judge?"

Attacking God is lucrative human-family business right now. Richard Dawkins' book *The God Delusion*, Christopher Hitchens' *God Is Not Great*, and Sam Harris's *Letter to a Christian Nation* all hit the bestseller lists. Their militant atheism sees Christianity not as a fallacy to be debunked but an evil to be resisted. Christians feel offended and many counterpunch rebuttals.

But how does Jesus respond?

Nothing.

He takes it. Like a sheep before the shearers, he shuts his mouth, says ancient prophecy. "Go to hell!" our culture screams at him. So he does, on our behalf.

Christopher Nolan's 2008 film *The Dark Knight*, based on the DC Comics character Batman, depicts the sorrow and cost of this true heroism.

At the story's climax, Batman defeats the diabolical Joker and Gotham lives to suffer another day. But in the final scene, Lieutenant Gordon laments that perhaps the Joker won after all. His demented genius had corrupted Gotham's rising star, District Attorney Harvey Dent. The Joker's deceit had driven Dent mad so that he became Two-Face, a new force of evil in Gotham.

Batman agrees that the knowledge of Dent's descent into Two-Face must remain hidden from Gotham. He then adds that the crimes of Two-Face must be blamed on Batman himself.

Nolan may not have consciously intended the connection, but the mythic parallels scream through the haunting night images in the film. Batman is Jesus, who according to the ancient texts not only bore the cumulative debris of the universe of human action but became that debris. In the words of the Bible, Jesus became sin. He never deserved bad Karma, but willingly took it upon himself so that by dying he might conquer death itself.

Hundreds of years before Jesus lived, the Jewish prophet Isaiah wrote about the anti-hero/hero who would turn history's final pages:

> There was nothing beautiful or majestic about his
> appearance,
>   nothing to attract us to him.
> He was despised and rejected—
>   a man of sorrows, acquainted with deepest grief.
> We turned our backs on him and looked the other way.
>   He was despised, and we did not care.
> Yet it was our weaknesses he carried;
>   it was our sorrows that weighed him down.
> And we thought his troubles were a punishment from
> God,
>   a punishment for his own sins!
> But he was pierced for our rebellion,
>   crushed for our sins.
> He was beaten so we could be whole.
>   He was whipped so we could be healed.

As the cops of Gotham begin their pursuit of Batman, Gordon confesses to his young son that Batman remains the hero Gotham deserves though not the hero it needs at the moment. To prevent the Joker from foiling Gotham's hope, Batman has turned himself into an outlaw, willingly carrying another's guilt.

They hunt Batman because he's willing to bear their fury. He's no hero; he's a silent and secret guardian, their scapegoat.

Today Jesus stands in as the butt of jokes and the scorned fool. What street preacher with a billboard reading "Jesus saves" hasn't ended up with rotten eggs or tomatoes on his face? But how else could the story go? The Dark Knight covers for crimes he didn't commit until the Day when all scores are finally settled. And that day will come. Until then, Jesus is Batman, as Batman is Jesus, submerged into the communal latrine of Gotham, our hometown.

TAKING EVERYTHING PERSONALLY

I sometimes scrounge through used bookstores, especially when I'm working on writing a project like this one. I get random ideas and inspirations, as I did a few weeks back when I found a dog-eared copy of Neal Cassady's *Grace Beats Karma*.

Perfect, I first thought. Then I wondered if someone in the publication pipeline had made a huge mistake. The cover shot couldn't possibly be a picture of Neal Cassady. It looked like someone had swapped cover photos with a book about behind-the-scenes gossip on the *Leave It to Beaver* show.

Supposedly, the photo had been taken just before the Cassady family left for church on Easter morning 1957. Neal is wearing a coat and tie and he's standing beside his three tidy children, Jami, Cathy, and John. It looks like the quintessential snapshot of 1950s domestic bliss, which is why I doubted its authenticity; Neal Cassady was no Ward Cleaver.

I grew up in the social back draft stirred up by Cassady's wild, magical life. Santa Cruz sits uneasily atop the San Andreas Fault on the north shore of Monterey Bay, about seventy miles south of San Francisco, a "quaking" sector of the planet, especially during the 1960s. At the time, I couldn't understand my hometown. But years later when I read about Cassady, things began to make more sense. Santa Cruz, with its beaches and redwood forests, had been my playground. As a boiling caldron of hip, it was also Neal Cassady's playground.

They called him the Holy Goof, the Father of Beat, the Primal Hippy. He lived fast, always sticking his thumb—and middle finger—in the eye of "The Man." Allen Ginsberg, Jack Kerouac, Tom Wolfe, and Ken Kesey each credited Cassady with inventing the stream of consciousness voice prevalent in their writings. In return they granted Cassady immortality in the poetry, novels, and films of the Beat movement of the 1950s and the psychedelic revolution of the 1960s.

In Kerouac's novel *On the Road*, Cassady is Dean Moriarty, the automobile driver with a Zen-like sense of the road. The "real" Cassady actually drove a bus for Ken Kesey's Merry Pranksters on their psychedelic tour across America. Tom Wolfe's book *The Electric Kool-Aid Acid Test* immortalized Cassady, the Pranksters, and their "Happenings"—light shows with rock music and free doses of LSD. Kesey himself wrote a tribute to Cassady shortly after Cassady's death in 1968, in a short story called "The Day After Superman Died." And the Grateful Dead gave him a song: "That's It for the Other One."

Cassady's Karma debt came due in 1958, when he was arrested for selling marijuana to an undercover cop.

Determined to make an example of him and to punish him for his public defiance, officials sentenced him to ten years in San Quentin Prison. It was from his prison cell that he wrote the letters that comprise the book *Grace Beats Karma*.

The prim photo on the cover of the book does not fit the image of Cassady, but it is authentic. Evidently there was a second soul inside the shell of this roving, rambling womanizer: a Neal Cassady who could don a suit and take his children to church. For all Cassady's rampaging foolery, he seemed to understand that he'd spent himself into a moral debt he could never hope to repay. In the title he seems to be declaring bankruptcy and appealing to the One who could "beat" his rap.

Sadly, Cassady's grace reprieve was short-lived. Grace brought him pardon but not the power to sustain a new life. He never escaped the gravity of the mass of bondage he'd accumulated around himself. After his parole, Cassady returned to his turbulent ways. He died beside a railroad track in Mexico in February 1968, the victim of a toxic reaction to barbiturates washed down with alcohol.

With grace Cassady might have found a reprieve from Karma, but he needed more than a reprieve; he needed a relationship with Someone stronger and more ingenious than himself. We all do.

"Karma gives me an orderly world," Andrew said.

"Does it? Is it really the only way to explain things?" I asked.

"The only way for me."

"As I see it, we have two possible worlds," I said, echoing a distinction I had learned long ago from E. Stanley Jones.

"Either Karma is sovereign and we have no appeal against its exactness, or a Person is sovereign, the One who makes choices and has power to implement them. This Person would either respond to our appeals or not."

When the bell sounded at 3:45 AM, the pilgrims who had come to Mahatma Gandhi's ashram in Sabarmati, India, rose and silently processed to the riverbank to say their prayers. In 1927, E. Stanley Jones stayed there with Gandhi eight days, and each morning joined the prayer march under the stars. The experience had a profound impact on him. In *Christ at the Round Table,* Jones recalls listening to the droning chants, then the quaint, sad voice of Gandhi expounding on the *Bhagavad Gita.* Jones marveled that such a slight man, wearing only a homespun loincloth—wielding nothing more than his own personal discipline, good will, and a strategy of nonviolent civil disobedience—could command such power, a power he imagined might one day bring the mighty British Empire to its knees.

Following one of these prayer walks, Jones approached Gandhi to tell him about the Round Table gatherings. Gandhi seemed intrigued and agreed to have a similar heart-to-heart conversation with Jones. Jones kept confidential most of the intimate details of their discussion, but he did relay one telling exchange.

Gandhi began. "The more I empty myself, the more I discover God," he confessed. "The world is a well-ordered machine, and we may discover God in obeying its laws, but no miracles are to be expected, and it may take ages." Gandhi then went on to acknowledge that he hadn't yet found spiritual enlightenment. Jones recalled reading a steely determination in the pundit's eyes, something he called "noble despair," as if he had braced himself for a long, uncertain struggle.

When Jones returned to his own cottage near the compound's spinning room, Gandhi's words haunted him. *"The world is a well-ordered machine. . . . No miracles are to be expected. . . ."* Was this the best hope from the best of men? If Mahatma, the "Great Soul," had not found enlightenment, what hope had an ordinary man?

Jones recalled his own experience. Twenty-five years before, he too had felt bankrupt and despaired of ever reaching God. Then he'd given his soul to Christ, a Person, not a machine. At that moment a miracle happened. He knew it. It had not taken ages. It had taken only an instant of surrender, a simple exchange of life for life. The next day Jones met Gandhi again and shared this story. The two men walked and talked and wept together, yet each out of a very different state of heart.

Karma exists, Jones concedes. The world is in fact a well-ordered machine. But mechanics need not define the baseline. The "Karma machine" might have a Designer, Someone with a will independent of the design itself. The "Everything" behind everything could be a Person. Seeing things this way gives the world a very different look and feel.

It did for Abraham Lincoln.

Like many, I have stood inside the Lincoln Memorial in Washington DC muttering under my breath the words etched on its marble walls. The words are Lincoln's and mark two of the most profound political declarations ever uttered. The Gettysburg Address frames the staggering human cost of the quest for justice and liberty; the Second Inaugural Address frames the spiritual meaning of that quest.

Washington DC March 4, 1865: A worn and aging president approached the temporary podium on the steps of the renovated Capitol. Lincoln's surprising election four years before had sparked a bloody civil war. After forty-eight embittering months he now stood before Federals and Confederates alike to interpret the catastrophe. Why had the conflict lasted so long and cost so many lives? Why had so many errors in judgment plagued each side?

Lincoln needed only 703 words to deliver his convictions, the shortest inaugural address in American history. *The London Spectator*, which had always criticized Lincoln in the past, called it "the noblest political document known in history."

His answers rang out stern and dreadful yet subtly comforting: God had willed it. The war continued, Lincoln said, because "the Almighty has his own purposes." This horror, he supposed, had come as recompense and a purging fire on a nation built upon a foundation of injustice: the rancor of slavery.

> Fondly do we hope, fervently do we pray, that this mighty scourge of war may speedily pass away. Yet if God wills that it continue until all the wealth piled by the bondsman's two hundred and fifty years of unrequited toil shall be sunk, until every drop of blood drawn with the lash shall be paid by another drawn with the sword, as was said three thousand years ago, so still it must be said "the judgments of the Lord are true and righteous altogether."

Strange words coming from Abraham Lincoln, who when he entered the White House did not confess an orthodox Christianity. As a young man his philosophy evolved away from his parents' Calvinism. After reading Thomas Paine's

Age of Reason, Lincoln adopted the Rationalism, Stoicism, and Deism of Enlightenment thinkers. History was not authored by the will of a personal God, but determined by the law of cause and effect. Things happened; they were not designed. Lincoln, in other words, believed in Karma, perhaps without the subsidiary doctrine of reincarnation.

The war broke Lincoln's Rationalism as completely as it broke his nation. As disaster upon disaster mounted, he could not logically explain the blundering, bloody, barbaric chaos as the consequence of cause and effect. Some "Purposeful Hand" seemed to be at work. God had taken sides—against both sides—and from the ash heap, Lincoln could hear his grieving, angry sobbing.

The experience transformed Lincoln from a man who believed in the "well-ordered machine" to one who openly appealed to the personal God for pardon, for help, and for solace.

"Now, at the near end of three years struggle the nation's condition is not what either party or any man devised or expected," Lincoln conceded. "God alone can claim it."

Just forty-one days before an assassin would end his life, Lincoln comes full circle, returning to the faith he'd long since rejected. He returns carrying his broken nation with him to a God who takes things very, very personally.

"I don't want to live in an arbitrary world," Andrew answered flatly. "Living at the whim of a tyrant is worse than hell—been there, done that."

A fire burned beneath Andrew's words. I recalled his earlier allusions to his father. I decided to risk a deeper question. "You couldn't trust your father?"

Andrew stared at me. What different lives we had lived; what different fathers we had been given. "Monomaniacal madman," he said. "One day he'd up and say, 'We're moving to Kansas.' Then he'd fall into a funk and call my mom a loser and say she was out to ruin his dreams. Then he'd disappear for a few days, then come back and act as if nothing had happened. He was like a crazy judge with absolute power."

Judge Roy Bean, I thought. I'd done a book report on Roy Bean when I was kid. I had to repress a smile; Andrew's case was anything but funny.

But Bean was a certifiable nutcase, and as the duly elected justice of the peace for Pecos County, Texas, from 1882 to 1902, Bean's word was law. "Hang 'em first, try 'em later!" he'd bark. He never did complicate justice with due process.

Bean presided from a saloon named the Jersey Lilly in the railroad tent city of Langtry, pitched on a bluff above the Rio Grande. The saloon and the town were both named after the love of Bean's life, Lillie Langtry, a British actress he'd never met. He'd hung a crusted picture of Miss Lillie behind his bar. And above the door he posted signs proclaiming "ICE COLD BEER" and "LAW WEST OF THE PECOS." From that "bar" of justice Bean and his tamed black bear bailiff dispensed liquor and a personalized and quirky version of legal righteousness.

Bean often sat on the porch of his saloon, rifle in hand, waiting for "customers" to find their way into his lair. His favorite victims were railroad passengers, desperate to find something to drink during their train stop in Langtry. Bean would serve them, and then stall for time before returning their change. When the train's warning whistle blew, the travelers would demand what was owed them, often with a few choice words. Bean would then fine them the exact amount for insubordination and send them cursing back to their railroad car.

Karma runs things with ruthless fairness. A person runs things with discretion. There's danger either way. We value judges in our system because they can deliver justice with individualized consideration. A judge with virtue can consider extenuating circumstances and apply laws with mercy. Without virtue, such power creates characters like Roy Bean and Andrew's father. I wondered again, *Which world would I prefer?* and I tried imagining growing up with Roy Bean as master of the house.

Maybe accepting a personal view of God came easier for me because I grew up with a father who let me into his world and welcomed and sometimes yielded to my appeals. For Andrew, the prospect dredged up other darker fears that made him reject the prospect outright.

In one sense Andrew had it right. The universe does act as its own law enforcement officer, judge, and jury. If I jump off a five-story building, I don't break the law of gravity; it breaks me. Gravity can't be defied and it doesn't have to arbitrarily decide to break my ankle. That just "happens," and the reason it happens is the law of gravity. Gravity might be manipulated by the curvature in an airplane wing, but if that plane stalls out in midair, gravity gets the last word. This kind of Karma is nonnegotiable.

Still Karma cannot explain everything. When good things happen to bad people and bad things happen to good people, when civil wars grow worse than they should, causes and effects don't seem to add up. Another personal factor has to be fitted into the equation. A whim, a decision, a will. Who this "personal factor" is and how humans relate to him remains the cosmic question. We've painted many faces for this personal God. Most of them bear a striking resemblance to our more visible and familiar authority figures.

In Detroit, Michigan, five times a day—dawn, noon, midafternoon, sunset, and before retiring—Abu al-Hajj falls to his knees, bows in the direction of Mecca, Saudi Arabia, and touches his leathered face to the earth. One billion Muslims around the world join Abu. It is called *Salat*, Muslim worship; a form of prayer to Allah and one of the five primary pillars or obligations of Islam. Salat consists primarily of phrases of praise to Allah, reiterating again and again a sworn, absolute submission to his will.

On Friday, the Muslim holy day, Abu visits his mosque to join the imam, or worship leader, in a service of chanting, kneeling, bowing, and standing. It's a fifteen-hundred-year-old liturgy that often includes the following prayer:

> God is greater. Glory be to thee, O God, and praise.
> Blessed is Thy Name and transcendent Thy majesty.
> There is no god but thee. I turn my face to Him who
> gave being to the heavens and the earth in true devotion.
> Not for me the fellowship of false worship. Truly my wor-
> ship and my oblation, my living and my dying, are God's
> alone, the Lord of all being. For there is no god beside
> Him. So is it laid upon me as one who is surrendered.

Surrender marks a Muslim's piety. The word *Islam* means "submission" or "surrender." Allah is a personal being, the only God who governs all natural and invisible affairs. Abu's primary duty is to yield body and soul to Allah's will. Salat is the five-times-per-day spiritual discipline drilling home this fact. Every human is utterly subordinate to Allah. Allah takes no counsel. He is bound to no oaths. He is and does whatever he decides to be and do.

Allah has no obligation to respond to Abu. Abu is a slave, Allah is master. Yes, he is "compassionate, merciful, peaceful, and sublime." Yet he never justifies himself. The chief end of Abu's life is to submit under Allah's purpose, whether it seems capricious or benevolent. Abu does not appeal for change; he yields to something that is already decided.

Andrew would never call himself a Muslim, but his image of God as dictator somewhat echoes Abu's theology. Abu submits to this god; Andrew would not, and chose instead another more predictable form of tyranny—Karma.

On the surface, Islam and Andrew's version of Karma seem light-years apart. Islam is monotheistic. Allah is personal and outside creation. Karma by contrast is pantheistic. All is One. "Spiritual" elements in the world are part of a whole that is governed by a clockwork system of cause and effect.

Yet these two religious frameworks share one common linchpin. Both are built upon resignation. Islam says "surrender"; Buddha says "surrender." In both, we humans remain powerless in the face of unbending determinism. Muslims concede to the determination of an unbending will. Buddhists concede to the determination of the clockwork universe. Either way, "Whatever will be will be."

Ancient Hebrews also believed in a personal Creator, but they framed his character in radically different terms. Their God stands beyond his creation, but he also interacts with his handiwork, especially humans, the objects of his greatest affection. Hebrews claim God invites real communication. He even welcomes appeals. Based on rules of engagement he reveals himself to everyone; he even promises to respond to those appeals and make changes in the imposition of his power.

This vision gives Jews a playful, reverential, and sometimes quarrelsome relationship with God. The Old Testament is peppered with stories of men and women who dared to challenge their God. Jeremiah, Job, David, and Moses all vow loyalty to God, but they all feel perfectly free to argue with him directly about how he's chosen to run the world around them. They even demand change. These Hebrews held a paradoxical, familial relationship with God, the way a child dearly loves yet pushes against her parents.

Jacob, an ancestral hero of Jewish people, even wrestled with God, literally. It's a strange story that comes down to us in the book of Genesis. One night an angel representing God himself appears to Jacob. Instead of shrinking in fear, Jacob tackles the messenger and begins demanding a blessing.

Jacob's name in Hebrew means "heel catcher," a play on words reflecting the strange circumstances of his birth (he came out of the womb holding the heel of his twin brother, Esau) and his Machiavellian personality. Jacob repeatedly "caught the heel" of people he wanted to plunder. He victimized his brother (Esau), his father-in-law (Laban), and even his own father (Isaac). By going hand-to-hand in a wrestling match with God, Jacob attempts to trip up God and snatch for himself some kind of divine advantage.

And what is God's response to Jacob's audacity? Does God evaporate him into the dust from whence he came? No. The angel merely cripples Jacob's hip—presumably to give him a permanent reminder of who is ultimately in charge. Then . . . surprise! God grants Jacob's plea by changing his name. Names invoked destiny. Jacob the scoundrel becomes Israel, which means "the one who struggles with God and overcomes." This scene establishes a stunning precedent for the kind of intimate relationship God invites!

Jews still embrace Jacob's/Israel's chutzpah in dealings with God. In the Broadway musical *Fiddler on the Roof*, Tevya, a Jewish Russian peasant, debates God while milking his cow. The scene is comical and yet profoundly personal.

> Dear God, you made many poor people. I realize, of course, that it's no shame to be poor. But it's no great honor either! So what would have been so terrible if I had a small fortune?

Tevya then breaks into song: "If I were a rich man . . ." His musical prayer ends,

> God who made the lion and the lamb,
> You decreed I should be what I am,
> Would it spoil some vast eternal plan
> If I were a wealthy man?

Tevya engages God with candor and humor, as intimate friend. He knows full well the promise of prosperity God gave his ancestors and wonders aloud, "So what about me?"

Jews and their spiritual grandchildren, Christians, see the "Everything" behind everything as personal. In a book I wrote with Jennifer Schuchmann, *Six Prayers God Always Answers*, we quoted G. K. Chesterton from his book *Orthodoxy*. I repeat it here because he makes this point splendidly:

The thing I mean can be seen . . . in children, when they find some game that they specifically enjoy. A child kicks his legs rhythmically through excess, not absence, of life. Because children have abounding vitality, because they are in spirit fierce and free, therefore they want things repeated and unchanged. They always say, "Do it again," and the grown-up person does it again until he is nearly dead. For grown-up people are not strong enough to exult in monotony.

But perhaps God is strong enough to exult in monotony. It is possible that God says every morning, "Do it again" to the sun; and every evening "Do it again" to the moon. It may not be automatic necessity that makes all daisies alike; it may be that God makes every daisy separately, but has never got tired of making them.

Because God takes everything he does personally, nothing is final or fixed. We can ask him anything, and he promises to respond.

We can offload cataclysmic concerns, like the mother of a soldier in combat kneeling in a silent church, pleading with God for protection, or a city begging for protection against a deadly epidemic. We can also pester him about small things, like a child folding her hands at mealtime and praying for her puppy's sore paw. Here Karma does not have the last word; God has the last word, because God entertains appeals delivered within the bounds of stipulations. Jews and Christians believe they can change God's mind; God in turn can change the course of reality. God cannot be manipulated, but he can be convinced.

If the stories in the Bible are any indication, God seems to respect most those who pursue him most aggressively, even those who refuse to take no for an answer. Jesus once told a story about a man who receives a late-night guest.

When he discovers he has no food (in that culture, a shameful position for a host), he goes to a neighbor and knocks on his door asking to borrow some provisions. His neighbor answers that he's too tired to get up. But the would-be host is desperate. He keeps knocking and pleading. Finally, to shut him up, the neighbor gets out of bed, opens his cupboard, and gives his friend the food he requests. Jesus credits the man's audacity and uses the story as a lesson for how we should address God. "Be audacious with God," he's saying.

I have a friend with a young daughter crippled by a form of cerebral palsy. Medically, the condition is not treatable. But every morning and every evening my friend kneels beside her child and prays, asking specifically for a complete healing. She uses all the medical understanding she has acquired when framing her prayers. She asks specifically and persistently, boldly and audaciously. And she has seen some unprecedented improvements. Not total healing, but some.

She asks and she keeps on asking. I dared once to wonder aloud how she could continue appealing when the results seemed to come so slowly. "Because one day my daughter will walk," she answered without hesitation. My friend is very sane. She is simply living out a faith that is honestly rooted in promises from God that she takes quite seriously. They give her the courage to impose and the hope to believe he'll respond. Karma isn't final for her. She keeps asking for an exemption.

Muslims confess that Allah is almighty; Jews and Christians say the same about Yahweh, the God of the Bible. Buddhists believe that all action has a cause and is a cause; Christians and Jews hold this same view of the world as well.

In reality, we Christians hold together the truths of both assertions—that God is almighty and the world works in a logical way—with the blended epoxy of a living, dynamic *relationship* with God, a relationship consisting of real-time interaction in prayer that dares to try to influence the Sovereign's governance of the world.

Ask a Christian, and she'll say this human/divine conversation converges finally in the life and death of Jesus of Nazareth. Jesus himself "puts God on the spot," promising repeatedly that God will respond to our appeals. He makes audacious claims about God's character and his willingness and ability to intervene individually in our lives and to change the world for our benefit. He likens God to a loving father who responds personally to his child's appeal.

> "Keep on asking, and you will receive what you ask for. Keep on seeking, and you will find. Keep on knocking, and the door will be opened to you. For everyone who asks, receives. Everyone who seeks, finds. And to everyone who knocks, the door will be opened."

"I believe God really listens to me and changes things," I said.

"I've prayed before. But what is it they say? 'God helps those who help themselves.' Rings true to me," Andrew responded.

"I tested God once to see if I could measure his response to prayer," I said.

"You experimented on God?" Andrew said with a smirk.

"Essentially, yeah. It was my PhD dissertation research. I wanted to see if people who were prayed for secretly developed different attitudes. So I modeled an experiment on a study done by a medical doctor named Randolph Byrd.

Back in 1988, Dr. Byrd conducted a double-blind prayer experiment with heart patients in San Francisco. Half of his patients received regular treatment, while the other half had treatment plus secret prayer. In the end, the prayed-for patients were much healthier. I decided to use the same process to measure the impact of prayer on human communication."

"And . . ." Andrew waited for the punch line.

"I hopped aboard the multi-million-dollar train of the state of Minnesota's anti-tobacco education campaign. I had 236 public high school students in my study. All of them were being taught that smoking is bad for your health. I asked a group of people to secretly pray for half of the students by their first names, to ask God to make them receptive to truth. After thirty days I gave all 236 students a Center for Disease Control survey designed to measure whether or not they intended to use tobacco. I compared each group."

"Did it work?"

"I don't think prayer works. God works. Yes, the students we prayed for secretly were three times more likely to say they wouldn't smoke."

"You proved God?" Andrew chuckled.

"Evidence, not proof. When we looked at the statistics, we couldn't prove what happened or why. We could only see that *something* changed. I think God gave us a flash of insight, like lightning in the dark of night. But yeah, I believe God hears prayer and changes things."

Andrew paused. "Is he a good man then, your father?" he asked suddenly, and I knew this wasn't a random question. It tied together, in his mind at least, with the flow of our discussion.

I nodded.

"That's not my world. If I believed God was like a father, I'd never know what to expect. *You* can pray. I don't think I can."

"You can always pray to be able to pray," I said. "Trust can be earned, but I think it can also be given for free, as a kind of miracle. I think God can give you trust by giving you a new picture of what he's like by giving you a new picture of a father."

Andrew's eyes grew distant. What was happening behind them, I couldn't tell.

How does trust in God come? How had I learned that a personal God did not have to terrify me?

The dense smell of fresh blood filled my memory. I was almost four years old, about the age I started shaving with my father, and I stood in a garage watching him and his friends butcher and wrap the fresh venison they had just harvested. I remember it like yesterday.

Ten days before, my father had gone deer hunting in Utah. All week the weather had been hot and the hunting poor. After six days, not one member of the hunting party had even seen a deer. The last day, my father traveled to town and phoned my mother to tell her he would be starting home the following afternoon. She then informed him that I had prayed that he would come home with two bucks. He chuckled and told her to prepare me for disappointment.

But the next morning, a cold front blew down from the Cascade Mountains to the west. While shivering atop a ridge covered with sage and juniper, my father spotted a large buck. He pulled up his .30-06 and shot. Thirty seconds later, a second animal bounded through the brush. Two more shots. Two bucks felled.

As a child, I accepted the connection: I prayed; something happened. God heard. God changed things. I mattered.

Too good to be true? Too simple? Not if everything is personal, not if the Person behind the personal keeps his word. Today the antlers of those two deer hang in the office where I am writing the words of this chapter. On them hang the basis of my entire life.

I studied Andrew's face. "Somewhere back in your life, Andrew, God has done something good, something specific that proves he's trustworthy." I paused to register his reaction. "If you want to remember that one good thing, even see it for the first time, God can and will show it to you. He'll go back there with you, if you will ask. He's a better father than you can imagine. He's better than I can imagine too."

9

TO BOOT

Sometimes things do turn out better than we expect. I always liked Cracker Jacks as a kid, but I remember one box in particular; my first, I believe. I was probably five, and we were driving from Santa Cruz to Portland to visit my grandparents. We stopped for gas somewhere near Mount Shasta, and my father bought boxes of the caramel popcorn with peanuts for my sisters and me. We devoured them, sitting in the back backseat of our Oldsmobile Vista Cruiser. The popcorn alone was beyond description—but then, a surprise! As I poured the last kernels into my sticky hand, out dropped a little packaged toy.

Imagine that, a bonus! I never expected it. It doesn't happen often, but sometimes we get one good thing, then something more to boot.

"So it's all about alleviating guilt, this business with Jesus?" Andrew took our adventure down yet one more rabbit trail.

It dawned on me that our dialogue had no discernable rhyme and no clear progress. I probably expected that it would build toward some kind of climax, but that didn't seem to be happening. Random questions shifted with moods and varying degrees of openness and suspicion, remarkably sudden and surprising.

Andrew's comment puzzled me. At first I didn't know how I should respond. "I guess I consider cleaning the slate a pretty big deal in itself."

"As far as it goes," he said. "So as you see it, Jesus—what did you call him, 'the toxic dump of the universe'—gets my stuff. What then?"

"Forgiveness," I said tentatively.

Andrew shook his head as if I'd lost him.

"I don't mean pretending to forget," I explained. "Forgiveness actually changes reality. I believe Jesus moves the consequences of our actions, our Karma, and absorbs it all himself. That's forgiveness. So when God looks at my track record, Jesus gets blamed for it! History not only has been rewritten, it's been re-imprinted in the fossil record of the cosmos. God forgives and forgets, and his forgetting isn't merely an absentminded miscue—like today, when I forgot to turn off my headlights. God forgets by changing the cause and effect sequence."

"I don't get it," he said flatly.

"When God pulls out a single thread from the tapestry of history," I said with a second wind of energy, "say the thread I wove into Roxanne's life, God no longer sees my role in it because, frankly, my role no longer exists. I took Jesus' offer of an exchange of destinies. He now gets the blame that once belonged to me. And he paid the Karma debt for that blame two thousand years ago. If I now beat myself up about what I did to Roxanne and talk to God about it and say, 'Oh, I'm really sorry that happened . . . God scratches his head and says, 'Hmm, that's odd, I don't have any record that you were a part of that. . . . What was that again?' It's like calling a creditor to beg for mercy and time to pay, then hearing him say, 'Oh, you must have the wrong number. There's no record of your account. Have a nice day!' "

An almost manic inspiration flowed out of me and converged with words I hardly recognized. I realized how personal this insight was for me. I'd never thought of these things in quite this way before that moment, let alone said them aloud to someone. It's oddly humbling to catch yourself speaking something you know to be true but don't know until the idea takes form in syllables off your own lips. I felt like stepping back to take notes.

Months later, while doing research for this book, I found a quote by Bono where he explains Jesus and forgiveness in almost identical terms. Perhaps my inspiration wasn't perfectly original after all. No matter.

Michka Assayas, who is not a confessing Christian, in his book *Bono: In Conversation with Michka Assayas,* records an interview with Bono in which he discusses the implications, here and now, of the sacrificial life of Jesus.

> *Assayas:* . . . I am beginning to understand religion because I have started acting and thinking like a father. What do you make of that?
> *Bono:* Yes, I think that's normal. It's a mind-blowing concept that the God who created the universe might be looking for company, . . . but the thing that keeps

me on my knees is the difference between Grace
and Karma. . . . [A]t the center of all religions is the
idea of Karma. . . . Karma is at the very heart of the
universe. And yet, along comes this idea called Grace
to upend all that "as you reap, so you will sow" stuff.
Grace defies reason and logic. Love interrupts, if you
like, the consequences of your actions, which in my
case is very good news indeed, because I've done a lot
of stupid stuff.

Assayas: I'd be interested to hear that.

Bono: That's between me and God. But I'd be in big
trouble if Karma was going to finally be my judge. . . .
It doesn't excuse my mistakes, but I'm holding out for
Grace. I'm holding out that Jesus took my sins onto
the Cross. . . . The point of the death of Christ is that
Christ took on the sins of the world, so that what we
put out did not come back to us, and that our sinful
nature does not reap the obvious death.

Bono, of course, is one of the most recognized icons in the
world. In recent years, the lead singer of U2 has leveraged
his astounding status to become a potent political voice
and advocate for social justice. At any given moment, Bono
and his sunglasses might be spotted lampooning a rogue
third-world dictator, or serving soup at an inner city shelter,
or doing a benefit concert for a four-hundred-year-old pub
slated for demolition, or spewing challenges to the CEO
of a pharmaceutical company. Most remarkably, perhaps,
Bono builds his convictions on his forceful, consuming
faith in the reality of Jesus Christ. In fact, he sees himself as
Jesus' agent of revolution in the world.

Personal pardon matters to Bono. But the implications
don't stop with what he offloads. What he receives from
Jesus matters as much and gives him a capacity beyond

his own strength to engage with and change the world. As
Jesus in his ugly death becomes Bono, Bono here and now
becomes Jesus.

In retrospect, I believe this was Andrew's real question. Jesus can take up our "stuff"; what can we take up
of his, and how can his power change our lives and then
the world? As E. Stanley Jones put it, "Buddhism says that
life is suffering: What is is wrong. Hinduism says that life
is Karma: What is is right. But Jesus says life is exchange:
What is can be made right."

"So tell me," Andrew continued, "what's really in this for you?
What's the bottom line? Why be a Christian?"

"I guess it's a kind of cost/benefit analysis," I answered.
"The things I want most in life aren't things but states of
mind and emotion. I want true love, to experience it and
be able to give it away. I want peace of mind, relief from
the angst and dread that seems to be natural to my dispo-
sition. I want a purpose, a real reason to breathe and eat
and wake up and endure the blasted aging process. I want
to be able to succeed in the relationships important to me.
And I can't seem to do any of this. None of what I really
desire seems to come naturally to my soul. But when I open
up and give everything I have and am to Jesus, I can rid
my soul of my own futility and let him come inside to live
alongside me, within me. And there—here—he produces
all his qualities. I don't have them perfectly or completely,
of course, but I'm finding things happening in me that just
aren't natural. That benefit is worth the cost of giving him
ownership."

"That's the trade-off?"

"It is. He gets title to everything. But I get written into his will. Literally, I'm made a member of the family. I get refrigerator rights in my true Father's house."

"Back to that word again," he said with forced coolness.

I reminded Andrew that I had gone to high school with Anthony Robbins. "A few years ago I saw a billboard on the freeway with his picture and dates he was speaking in Minneapolis. I called his office to see if I could meet him while he was in town. His gig cost $1,500 a day. I wasn't going to pay that. But his secretary sent me a VIP pass for a front-row seat. I went. At a break, I went up to greet him. We shared a few memories. Then Tony sent an assistant to load me up with materials from his sales table: $1,000 worth of books and recordings."

"That's pretty amazing. He seems genuine," said Andrew. He leaned forward, eager to hear the rest of my tale.

"People at the seminar were ravenous for his wisdom. They cheered and shouted and danced like Pentecostals at a tent meeting when he came out on stage."

Andrew laughed. "I believe it. We did that too in our group sessions just watching videos."

"You explained his philosophy very well earlier, Andrew," I said. "Robbins is all about mastering your mental state—emotions, thoughts, behaviors. He installs specific physical triggers that make certain mental states automatic. If I want to feel passion, concentrate, or relax, I can literally snap my fingers in a certain way—"

"I know," he interrupted.

"I don't buy it," I said. "I don't believe Robbins is right. I don't think we humans are mere animals like dogs or mice that can be wired to make all our actions and emotions so easily controlled. I think the remarkable story of human achievement is also pockmarked with the persistent failure of our attempts to manage our mental states. We've tried countless systems and schemes—monasteries, meditation, brainwashing, electric shock, and every imaginable therapy. They all break down. Robbins 'wired' himself for the behaviors that supposedly generate great relationships. Has that worked out for him?"

"We're hopeless then?" Andrew answered back. "The skeptic always has a comeback argument."

"Yes and no," I replied. "I know I can't manage my mental state, but Jesus can. He really can. When I swap identities with him, he gets me and I get him. I don't have it in me, but he has it in him, and when he's in me, I have it in me. If he's perfect, then perfect power to live perfectly becomes available for me. Sure, I don't leverage his power perfectly, but it's very, very real."

Andrew studied me suspiciously.

"I'm experimenting with this," I explained. "From Robbins I learned to put myself in a mental state and register that state. I could identify what *passion* feels like. His techniques try to install that state through classic conditioning, like Pavlov ringing a bell to make his dog drool. What I do instead is invite Jesus to reveal one of his virtues in me so I can taste it and know it. His love has a certain flavor. So does his peace, joy, and kindness. I can't generate these virtues on my own. I just can't. Man, I don't have love and peace in me! But when I swap lives with Jesus, he comes and lives in me, and he can manifest his attitudes through my body, mind, and emotions. It happens. I'm discovering this. I can 'channel' Jesus' patience when that's what I need most. I know I'm not a patient person, but he is!"

"You're telling me you become a better person than you should be?" Andrew asked.

"Not perfect, but better, yes," I said. "The Bible talks about two kinds of life, using two words in the Greek language: *bios* is biological life, and *zoe* is spirit life. These are two different forces and energy sources. Calories fuel little fires in our bodies to feed our bios. Zoe needs alternative energy. We're like hybrid cars with dual engines. We can run on bios, but we're missing optimal performance if we don't burn zoe as well for our secondary engine. The Bible says that Jesus brings us this zoe—another fuel for living here and now and on into the next ten thousand years. Zoe is highly efficient and powerful and limitless in time. It generates states of living beyond what we humans typically experience in our biological lives. And it allows us to accomplish feats of power and focus. There are many stories of this both today and throughout history. Sometimes we call these miracles."

"So Jesus Karma gives us this zoe," Andrew said.

"I think so, but I think Jesus IS zoe itself," I answered. "I have felt his feelings, and sometimes I've even done things he did. I can feel when it isn't from me. I just can. Paul, one of the early Christian teachers, put it this way: 'I no longer live, but Christ lives in me.' I can relate, not always and not perfectly, but I have felt Jesus loving someone through me when I knew I had nothing of the sort on my own."

"How's this different from Buddha saying we're one with God?" Andrew turned again to catch sight of his mother.

"Actually, I think God always remains apart and somewhat distant from us, though he comes to live in us. He wants the distinction to remain—subject and object. Love wouldn't be possible without that distinction and separation. God said, 'Let there be light . . . and oceans . . . and elephants . . . and man and woman.' Until then, everything was God and God was everything. But Christians believe that when God created, God divided and made things distinct. There's something lonely and dangerous about this, but it makes giving and receiving love possible. How could God love selflessly if God was all there is?"

"So God hides from us?" Andrew asked with a hint of sarcasm. "Absence makes the heart grow fonder . . ."

I thought carefully before I answered. In my mind, I again saw my father lying motionless on his bed. I saw him pulling back toward his final drastic separation from me. The man who gave me a name—who let me chase him around the house shooting rubber bands at him, who taught me to throw a curve ball, to say my prayers, to take them seriously and believe that God takes them seriously—was pulling back. Again the sorrow almost paralyzed me.

Buddha once said that life is suffering and suffering comes through disappointment. If I cease desire, I cease to suffer. If I cannot care, I cannot be disappointed. But this seems to me like curing a headache with a guillotine. Instead of stuffing desire, Jesus teaches me to inflate it. He pushes me to care more, not less, to give my heart away and embrace the grief of all the separations I must endure in the process. Through separation I learn the value of relationships and the way of love.

My grandfather—my father's father—made his living as a farmer, a gambler, and a marksman, and at certain points in his life made nearly equal amounts of money in all three careers. He had a gunslinger's reputation spun into legends by his friends and then inflated later by my father and his nine brothers, who told and retold his feats at Herringshaw family reunions.

At age thirteen, my grandfather bet some friends he could shoot an apple off the head of a neighbor boy. He won the bet. He'd beg a silver dollar off a poker buddy, toss it into the air, and plug a hole through it with a .22 caliber rifle. If he missed, he'd pay a dollar of his own. If he hit it, he'd win the coin, then take the damaged goods to the bank and exchange it for a good one. He once won a twenty-five-pound turkey by hitting 499 out of 500 clay pigeons in an Ohio state shooting tournament. He was a straight shooter, my grandfather.

He also shot at my father—with his words. My father grew up the thirteenth of fourteen children and the ninth of ten boys. Early on he became the brunt of his father's caustic wit. Who knows why such things happen, why a man would torment his own son. It happens.

My father took to eating, and over the course of fifteen years wrapped himself—body and soul—in thick layers of insulation. He hated himself and, as he said later, he hated others around him. Along the way, he developed an explosive temper that he used to keep people at bay. His anger, of course, only made the cycle of rejection worse.

When he was fifteen, he went to visit his oldest brother, who had just lost his own teenage son to polio. The grief had led his brother to Jesus, and during the visit, on New Year's Eve, my father too exchanged his life with Jesus.

Things changed radically after that. He lost fifty pounds. The following fall he played football, and the next spring hit .400 on his high school baseball team. Somewhere along the way, a new force displaced his anger:

kindness. My father eventually became the kindest of men, certainly the kindest I've ever known. I don't think kindness came naturally to him; it came supernaturally. When he dumped his bitterness on Jesus, Jesus dumped kindness into him. That became a new identity. He developed a deep curiosity about people. He loved nothing more than to ask questions and then listen to their stories. Plain and simple, he liked people. Working with them as he did, they often disappointed and even hurt him. Sometimes they made him angry. But he always retained the same kindness—the kindness that was and yet wasn't his.

Years ago my father came to hear a lecture I gave on spirituality and the Christian faith. Afterward we sat down to talk. He was very kind, but plainly truthful.

"You're smart," he said. "That was an interesting talk. I learned a lot. I believe what you said is true." Then he reached his hand out and covered the back of mine. "But you don't. You don't believe what you said. There's no love in your words."

His words cut me like a surgeon's scalpel: a painful, necessary wound. As the years have passed, I've grown by fits and starts to find that love. A reservoir of kindness doesn't flow naturally from me. More often than not I miss windows of opportunity to express it. But once in a while, at surprising moments, something above and beyond me will take over. At such times my words and actions do become more and better than I could make them on my own. Jesus flows through.

Five summers ago we traveled with my parents to northern Michigan for a Herringshaw family reunion. The night before we returned home, I drove into town to buy gasoline. As I filled the tank, I glanced across the parking lot at someone standing at a pay phone. Above the hum of the pump, I thought I heard a cry or a shout, but I couldn't be sure.

After paying my bill, I drove across the lot toward the phone and rolled down my window. A man was now sitting beneath the phone, the receiver dangling above his head. I could hear him wailing.

"Can I help you?" I heard myself say. The moment I spoke, something in me wished I hadn't. I was tempted to drive off.

He looked up toward me. He was weeping. "My son . . ." His words were hardly audible.

I opened the door and walked toward him.

"My son was just killed in a car accident," he wailed.

I froze. My heart skipped a beat. Did I have time for this? Without more debate, I knelt there where he'd crumpled to the ground. As I did, he reached out and buried his head into my shoulder. He wept in big, convulsive sobs.

I once debated a Jewish religion professor in a public forum at a state university. He claimed to be a "radical pluralist" who believed that all individual perspectives depict a legitimate truth. He went so far as to say, "Jesus is Messiah . . . in your reality." I asked him if this meant that we were like two people looking at the Grand Canyon, one from the north rim and the other from the south. He said that he believed it was more radical than that. We each were living in our own reality, in essence looking at different canyons in different states using a phone call to span a very, very wide chasm. He said quantum physics means we create the very reality we expect, and that each is utterly personal. There are literally as many parallel universes as there are individuals.

At the time I was befuddled by his arguments and stumbled through a rote rebuttal that didn't really rebut anything he said. But afterward I thought about the argument and why it troubled me so. I wish now I could have recast my objections.

What I should have said is that I think that the world— or worlds—he describes would be terribly lonely. He might be right, but radical pluralism means radical aloneness—not the way I want to live. I could have asked him if he thought he could choose to share his own world with another. Could he choose to give up his own world and enter another's—for the sake of friendship and love? This was how I understood God. That in Jesus, God had relinquished his right to live in his own isolated dimension, and for the sake of friendship had entered my world, a world God has allowed me to create. He came into my world to in turn invite me into his. The cost, of course, to everyone involved in such a transaction must be staggering and bitter. Sharing life means sharing mutual desires, disappointments, and suffering. I had stumbled into another man's world and into his suffering.

The stranger beneath the pay phone began to weep out his story. His name was Greg. He lived in Detroit. He had come north on a fishing trip with his father and they were staying in a nearby motel. That evening he found a message slipped under his door asking that he call home. His elderly father had already fallen asleep, so he had walked down the street to find a phone.

The message was dire: His eighteen-year-old son, the pride of his life, had been killed that afternoon after rolling his pickup.

I listened, feeling numb and distant. We sat for maybe ten minutes. I tried to find words. None came. Inside I wanted to drive away and forget the matter, but then I berated myself for my coldness.

Greg collected himself. "I've got to go tell my dad." He rose to his feet, and I stood with him.

Then I heard my words, "I'll go with you. I'll help you tell him." Greg started to cry again. Suddenly, my cool pity for him turned to sorrow. My own emotions, so slow to respond, thawed and broke in a torrent. I felt Greg's heart, a father's heart. I imagined myself in his shoes, that one of my precious daughters or dear boys had been snatched from me.

I had stumbled in deep to the level that was no longer that of a mere observer. I had crossed an invisible line from being a stranger watching to someone bearing a part of the agony. I drove Greg down the street. Together we stood for a moment on the threshold of the motel room. Then we stepped through.

As we entered, Greg's father woke suddenly, as if he already knew. Greg cleared his throat, but no discernable words came forth. He fell to the floor, whimpering with new tears.

I stepped forward and spoke to the terror-stricken old gentleman. "Your grandson has been killed," I said softly. Then I sat on the edge of the bed and watched the two lumbering fishermen hug one another and wail and weep, pause for a few seconds, then begin again. Then from somewhere beyond my own limits, I found tears welling up in my eyes. I could not stop them, though I thought it foolish to let them go. This wasn't my tragedy. No matter: Someone had made it mine and had imposed on me sudden and terrible love; created, then knotted together by a suffering I could hardly imagine.

I stayed with Greg and his father until they had packed and loaded their truck for their dreary drive home. I asked if I could pray with them, for God's peace. They agreed. I wanted to say something, but didn't want to say it to them. What could I pretend to give? I simply talked to God in their presence and in their stead. That was all. I left them my phone number, and they drove away.

Still in a daze, I drove slowly back to sneak into the room where my own children slept soundly and safely. I knelt beside them, prayed again, and thanked God, not merely for their safety but for a new glimpse of his Father's heart, for counting me fit to share someone's sorrow.

One week later, I received a phone call from Greg. He sounded composed but weary. The funeral had come and gone. He told me details. Hundreds of friends and family had come. His son, he learned, had started attending a church. Greg said he needed to call me just to make sure I wasn't an angel. "I think I need God too," he said over the phone. "I think I need to find a new path."

Writing his story down, I once again feel the weight of sharing Greg's sorrow. It comes again, the same heavy, brokenhearted father's love. We shared that—Greg, me, and the true Father in heaven—for one bitterly sad moment, and now again when we all remember it.

I didn't ask for that sorrow; I came upon it and stayed around just long enough for God to break it over the top of me! Of course! What did I expect? When I gave Jesus my "stuff," he in turn gave me his "stuff"—many surprising delights, even some supernatural wonders and abilities. But he also gives me the privilege of carrying his love into little hidden corners of his world. To do that means embracing— not suppressing—sorrow. It means elevating desire, not killing it. As the apostle Paul once put it, "I want to know Christ and the power of his resurrection and the fellowship of sharing in his sufferings."

I took two deep breaths as I studied Andrew. I imagined my daughters and sons peppering me with questions much like Andrew had. I knew that my kids would need my attention and my heart more than my answers. From somewhere I hadn't expected, a warm compassion for Andrew enveloped me. All my answers meant less than my attentiveness, and the patience and attentiveness toward him had come from Someone outside of me.

"You asked me about the bottom line," I said. " 'Jesus gets my Karma; what do I get of his?' " I said, repeating what he'd said earlier.

Andrew nodded.

"Bottom line: the opportunity to love and to be loved." Once more the now familiar pulsebeat of loneliness and encroaching separation took hold of me. My father would soon leave this world. Yet I would remain, first and last, a son, and secondarily a father. Jesus gave this role to me in his Karma, and it remains the one preeminent and stunning benefit of sharing his identity.

Imagine that, a bonus. Bonuses don't happen often, but then, surprise! Sometimes we get one good thing, then something more to boot.

COMING CLEAN

It started with a polite reminder: "Pardon the intrusion, but please remit the payment stipulated. Thank you." I tossed the notice in the circular file.

The next came more to the point: "Pay, please!" This one I buried under a stack of junk mail.

Finally, a threat: "Pay your blasted bill, or our six-foot-eight, 325-pound credit counselor will come for a visit."

Debt collection is no fun, believe me.

I knew the game. I knew that what I'd wracked up would cost me big; and I knew my assets—I had nothing. I had nothing with which to pay this bill, because it wasn't money I owed. Money would have been far simpler. This was a more personal debt.

I owed justice.

My debt of justice was a matter of public record. A list of the charges is spelled out. I don't have to share details. Bottom line: I have added pain and disorder to the world, and because the world and the world's Maker demand justice, I was saddled with the bill.

But I could not pay.

So I did the only thing open to me: I ran for my life. I ran in many directions at once, taking on assumed identities, avoiding commitments, never staying still long enough to be discovered. I lived on the run until running and life seemed inseparable. But no matter how fast or how far afield I flew, I always ended up looking over my shoulder, awaiting my moment of reckoning, expecting it, but always dreading it, and so never willing to turn and face the judgment. I ran. I ran until the day . . .

Perhaps you understand. Maybe you know the dread of a debt you cannot repay. Everyone must pay his own debt. That's the law called *Karma*. We reap what we sow. Trouble is, we sow more trouble than we're worth. We run a deficit budget that only grows worse by the day. We've made a mess of things, a real and actual mess.

Karma happens.

Karma sucks.

Mine.

Yours.

And the Karma of every one of the 6,672,443,878 persons on the planet at the moment I'm writing this line.

That's a fact—the bad news before the good news.

I've never prescribed medicine, but I have been tempted to prescribe Johnny Cash. A time or two I've considered sending a counselee home with an assignment to spend a week listening to nothing but Cash's music. These were good people, who knew they were good, but perhaps imagined themselves to be a bit better than they actually were. There's nothing like a little Johnny Cash to slap a decent soul with a cold-fish dose of reality. I've never quite had the guts to do it, maybe because I know I should take that medicine a bit more myself. I could use a little more Cash in my life—the bad news so I can appreciate the good.

Johnny Cash was "The Boy Named Sue" and "The Man in Black." He did country, classic rock, blues, outlaw, folk, and gospel. Cash lived, well, Cash. For nearly six decades he rode the rail lines of his own deeply personal music—personal yet painfully public, a package that carried him several times in and out of popular acclaim, and under and then through a series of crippling addictions. Start to finish, Cash's music changed little, always depicting a man who longed to change himself but couldn't. Confession songs like "God's Gonna Cut You Down" and "The Beast in Me" expressed his rare, odd sanity in the purest sense of the word.

John Fraiser assesses Cash this way: "It's worse than any of us think. He's damned, you're damned, we're all damned, and there's [nothing] any of us can do about it." Cash lays bare his confession, and then demands anyone listening do the same.

But in the second half of his career, through brokenness and the tender nurture of his second wife, June Carter, Cash began to reach for grace. His ballads "Help Me," "I Came to Believe," and "Redemption" depict his receiving forgiveness from God and—amazingly—extending it to others as well as himself.

For Johnny Cash, it all happens in the right order—the bad news comes first. He understood God's labor in our lives to first awaken our conscience with a blaring declaration of his demands. God is perfect; we are not. Once we see our desperate plight beside this unachievable standard, we can begin to receive and hold his gift of grace. Before we can trade our Karma with Jesus, we have to know that we need to.

Knowing we have no other out is our last best hope.

NBC's *ER* proved to be one of the most successful series in the history of television, in part for its boldness in tackling issues not usually covered in prime time: religion, for instance.

In an episode titled "Atonement," number 13 of season 14, a prison doctor who gave lethal injections to prisoners on death row is dying of cancer and confronts a hospital chaplain (Julia) who has come to his bedside to offer him spiritual comfort. The prison doctor (Dr. Truman) wants no comfort and has no time for soft-soap platitudes of tolerance and inclusive faith. He wants the cold, hard facts. He wants to face his culpability.

> *Dr. Truman:* God tried to stop me from killing an innocent man and I ignored the sign. How can I even hope for forgiveness?
>
> *Julia:* I think . . . sometimes it's easier to feel guilty than forgiven. . . .
>
> *Dr. Truman:* I don't want to go on. Can't you see? I'm old. I have cancer. I've had enough. The only thing that is holding me back is that I'm afraid. I am afraid of what comes next.
>
> *Julia:* What do you think that is?
>
> *Dr. Truman:* No, you tell me. Is atonement even possible? What does God want from me?
>
> *Julia:* I think it's up to each one of us to interpret what God wants.

Dr. Truman: So people can do anything? They can rape, murder; they can steal, all in the name of God, and it's okay?

Julia: No. That's not what I'm saying.

Dr. Truman: (voice rising to a shout) Well, what are you saying? Because all I'm hearing is some New Age, God is love, one-size-fits-all crap!

Johnny Cash, Dr. Truman, me, maybe you: Hit me with the truth, ugly though it is! Only then, at our point of no return, can we stub our toe on the buried treasure before us. Only then can we stumble upon a reprise, a surprise!

This book has been a conversation about the mess we make and the possibility of one surprising solution.

Perhaps it is possible to swap our Karma, to deal with Jesus, who promises to assume our debt and grant us access to his merit and all the benefits that are included. All we have to do is agree to the terms, his terms.

My father visited Art Kuku occasionally on Friday mornings. He'd have breakfast early at the diner in Duxsbury, and then drive to Art's before heading to town to make hospital visits. In the four years he'd served as pastor of Danforth Church in the backwoods of east central Minnesota, he'd seen Art almost every month. This visit would be different.

He steered his car down the rutted gravel driveway. Around the last bend he spotted five of Art's dogs barking and cantering to greet him. In a clearing just off the driveway, he spotted fifteen more huddled around the carcass of one of Arne Swanson's dairy cows.

Art kept sixty-five dogs, most of which he called by name. The year before, the Minnesota Department of Natural Resources had shot twenty-seven of them for killing deer. It broke Art's heart and made him madder than a hornet. His dogs slept in one rusty trailer house. Art slept in another beside it.

"Art! Art, you around?" My father yelled as he stepped—carefully—out of his car. Dogs encircled him like a hurricane, sniffing his pant legs and spraying the tires.

The trailer door swung open and out shuffled an old man hunched over in a pair of stained overalls. "Get away from him, you mongrels!" he barked. Then he moved with surprising grace down the steps, kicking at two puppies playing with his shoelaces.

"Pastor Howard! You're late." Art extended his hand. He was eighty-five years old and ailing, but his mind was keen. He still repaired two-stroke engines for spending money and taxes. Traces of grease could be seen in the crevices of his palms. My father extended his hand in return.

"Come on in." Then he added, "I'll bet you want your suit back. And you probably want to know why I didn't come back to church last week."

"You can keep the suit. It doesn't fit me anymore."

"Truth be," Art chuckled, "I didn't get around to getting cleaned up. I didn't dare come looking like this." Art rubbed his hands against his bristled cheeks, then ran his fingers through his thick and matted hair. He smiled, deliberately showing off gray and missing teeth.

Art hadn't stepped foot in a church since his wedding day in 1932. When he walked in the doors of Danforth Church Sunday morning two weeks before, scrubbed and shaved and sporting a borrowed blue suit, hardly anyone recognized him. Once they did, everyone laughed and slapped him on the back and invited him to stay for the potluck. Art was the life of the party that day.

He'd come clean quite by accident. On Monday morning that week he'd felt chest pains. With no phone to call for help, he crawled onto his ATV and drove himself twelve miles to Sandstone Hospital. The doctor on duty told him he was suffering a heart attack and admitted him immediately.

Later that week, after his heart had stabilized, two nurses conspired to get him into a bathtub, scrub him head to foot, shave him, and cut his hair. He objected, mostly out of modesty, but they prevailed. It was his first thorough cleaning in decades. When my father visited him on Friday in the hospital, Art seemed quite pleased with himself.

"Maybe I'll come to church if they let me out of here on Saturday," Art boasted.

"You're welcome anytime. You always have been," answered my father.

"Can I borrow a suit? You're about my size."

My father laughed. "You don't need a suit to come to Danforth Church."

" 'Course I do."

"If they let you out tomorrow, I'll have a suit for you."

Art went home the next day. Sunday morning he rode his ATV to church, walked in neat and tidy, sat in the fifth row, sang the hymns, listened to the sermon, and stayed for the potluck.

Then Art went home. The following Sunday he didn't return. Most people wondered why. My father understood. The following Friday he drove out to see him again.

My father and four dogs followed Art into his trailer house. The room, as always, was as tattered as Art himself.

"I made extra strong coffee, thinking you might show up," Art boasted. He stroked his face again. He hadn't shaved since the Monday after he'd been to church. His thick whiskers stood up off his face like tight rows of white-washed fence posts.

"You're welcome back anytime."

"Oh, don't fool yourself. They don't want me there, not lookin' and smellin' like this," Art chuckled.

My father didn't argue his point. He had been in Danforth long enough to know the truth. Art would be welcome as long as he would come clean.

"It's time I ask, Art. You had a close call with that heart attack. The doctors say you could have another. It's a matter of time. Are you ready to die?"

"You tell me," he said with a note of defiance.

"You've read the Bible?" my father asked.

"Can't read," said Art. "But I watch some of those TV preachers." Then he paused and grew pensive.

"My mother was a praying woman. I loved my mother. I dream of her sometimes. She loved animals. She taught me to love animals and pray to God."

"Are you ready to meet him?"

Art put down his coffee and stared out the grease-splattered kitchen window. "I've done some ugly things in my life, things that chased away my beautiful wife and my children. That was long ago. I lived many years with regrets. I came out here to escape. That never worked."

Art paused and lifted his eyes to my father's. They were both silent a moment more. Then Art continued.

"Then one Sunday I was watching one of those preachers. He talked about coming to Jesus and coming clean, to get clean. He put some words on the screen. I don't remember them, but he said if I would repeat those words and mean it, God would hear and do the rest. That was that. I did it. I said those words. Know what? It happened. Next minute, I felt like all the muck of all my life had washed away in a river I couldn't see, but I sure could feel."

Art paused again. "So you tell me, preacher, am I ready to meet God?"

"You are," my father answered softly. He reached out and took hold of the old man's arm. "Ready as you can be."

"Good. Because I don't suppose I'll bother getting dolled up for church again, except when they bury me. Sure you don't want your suit back?"

"No."

"Then bury me in it," Art chuckled. "And they can clean me up and shave me if it will make them feel better."

Making the trade is that simple, as simple as honest-to-God simple prayer.

Andrew stood abruptly, nodded, and without another word turned to go. He paused for just a moment, as if waiting for me to object. I smiled and thanked him and said something I can't now recall, something about how I hoped our time had been meaningful to him. I said something too about how what he had said had helped me see things in new ways. He nodded again, and then walked toward the exit at the back of the room.

I didn't say anything more and I have not seen or spoken to him since.

I don't know if our conversation stayed with Andrew or if it changed him the way it changed me.

I didn't try to stop him. Jesus didn't either. He let Andrew walk, the way he lets any seeker walk. The Gospels tell the story of a curious young man who peppers Jesus with questions, the same sort of questions Andrew leveled at me. Jesus gave him the bad news first, the ultimatum: "Sell everything and join me," Jesus said. But the young man had a lot to lose. He had money and position and security. He chose to walk away. And Jesus, who knew his potential and his destiny, who could have used his power to bend the lad's will, did nothing. He didn't want a slave; he wanted a friend, so he let him walk.

Maybe that young man reconsidered. Maybe. I have my doubts. Moments and tipping points of decision tend to come quickly and pass quickly. Lightning flashes for an instant in the black of the night, and for that moment everything is clear. Then the flash dissolves and darkness returns. Andrew and I had a flash moment when the paths down both forks of the road came clear. Then that instant passed. Does lightning strike twice in the same place? In Andrew's case, I can only hope and pray it does.

Jesus tells another story of a wealthy father who has two sons. The younger asks for his inheritance while his father is still living. In that society such a request was tantamount to saying, "Father, I want you dead!" Yet instead of retaliating, the father releases half his estate to him. The younger son then goes abroad and squanders the treasure on prostitutes and rogue living. Eventually the impoverished boy comes to his senses and heads home again, hoping to be accepted as one of his father's servants. The father, who has been watching for his son every day since his departure, sees the boy walking down the road toward him and runs out to meet him, throws his arms around him, and commands his servants to prepare a great feast. Without shame, the father brings the boy back into full relationship. He is a son and an heir again.

The nature of total forgiveness seems to be wrapped in total forgetfulness. God forgets.

As we have seen in the preceding pages, this deliberate forgetfulness had a cost. God buried the toxins of all time deep inside the heart of Jesus, his son, who takes the waste products to hell itself—to a place somehow and somewhere out of the universe, where it disappears into the infinity of his goodness. The heart of Jesus is that wasteland where God seems to remove from history all the crimes, small and great. His forgiveness doesn't change facts; it reassigns responsibility for them—from me and you to Jesus.

The first followers of Jesus explained this process by saying that Jesus went to Hades on our behalf. Like the epic heroes in the great stories, he passed through the underworld by his own voluntary death. But because he suffered unjustly, and suffered for Karma not his own, death could not hold him. His death was the death of death itself.

There in the caverns of hell, Jesus "dumped" what he bore on our behalf and then returned to life.

That's how the story goes. . . .

But when he returned, he retained the scars of his feat. As Frodo in Tolkien's *Lord of the Rings* bore forever the haunting pain of the knife wound he suffered at the hand of the Nazgul Wraith-King on Weathertop, so Jesus retains the scars of his death on the Roman cross to remind all creation of the cost of love and forgetful forgiveness.

Forgetful grace doesn't seem fair because it is not fair. It counters Karma justice, a knowledge of which we carry in genetic code. The older son in Jesus' story of the prodigal holds out for fairness and stands embittered by his father's mercy. Grace makes a scandal of justice. He complains that his father had never thrown a feast for him, though he had remained faithful in the family covenant. The father responds (and this is Jesus' second point), "Everything in my estate has always been yours. You could have asked for anything at any time!" Ask! Jesus is saying, because you have a relationship with your Father God.

Asking matters. It makes a difference.

David the King of Israel heard a knock at his chamber door. It was Nathan the prophet. The last time David heard from Nathan, the seer brought good news—great news, in fact. David wanted to build a new house for the worship of God. God sent Nathan to tell David that he approved the plan and that David's family would carry on the kingship of Israel.

But this time things were different. Nathan entered and he wasted no time. He began by telling a story. David listened carefully. Nathan told him of a rich man who had stolen a sheep from a poor man. David, thinking the story was an actual account, grew furious. He demanded justice. Nathan stared at him and said, "You're the man!"

The story had been a fable that paralleled what David had done. David had secretly stolen Bathsheba, the wife of Uriah, one of his most faithful captains. Then to cover Bathsheba's pregnancy, he had arranged to have Uriah killed on the field of battle. The crime seemed to be concealed. But it was not concealed from God. Nathan learned the truth directly from God and on behalf of God, rebuked David.

At the moment of truth, David could have gone in either of two directions. He could have bolted and hidden from God or turned to God. He asked for mercy and pardon. The exposure to bad news and its dire truthfulness melted David's heart. He broke, and in a torrent of grief poured out his regret and his plea for pardon. A poet by nature, David put pen to his confession in the painful but honest Psalm 51. In these words he asks for pardon, plain and simple:

> Have mercy on me, O God,
>   because of your unfailing love.
> Because of your great compassion,
>   blot out the stain of my sins.
> Wash me clean from my guilt.
>   Purify me from my sin.
> For I recognize my rebellion;
>   it haunts me day and night.
> Against you, and you alone, have I sinned;
>   I have done what is evil in your sight.
> You will be proved right in what you say,
>   And your judgment against me is just.

Most everyone prays. According to recent research, more than 90 percent of Americans say they pray. We don't always know how, and few of us feel confident, but we try. Especially in a pinch, we call out for help to Someone out there.

Swapping Karma with Jesus begins with a simple, honest-to-God appeal in the form of prayer. It is the "big ask."

Jesus no longer lives physically on earth, but many of us believe he still lives in the words he left behind and in the lives of those who believe in him. He grants special access to God the Father and is with us by the mysterious presence of his Holy Spirit, who is everywhere, enabling us to talk with Jesus at any time.

The Holy Spirit plays the role of message transmitter and translator. We speak out in plain English (or whatever language we're most comfortable with), and he carries our ordinary words that don't seem to leave the room right to the essence of the presence of God, who listens to every word and responds with a message of his own.

When our prayers contain a request to take God up on his offer to swap Karma, to exchange destinies with Jesus, God's response is instantaneous. He's already made the investment himself. He's just waiting for takers. When we express interest and then willingness, the contract instantly activates. In fact, the legal department of heaven has already drawn up papers with my name and yours, and filled in the lines with Jesus' signature in blood on the bottom. When we make the call, the contract is sealed. His Word and ours make it signed, sealed, and delivered.

So how can you address God with the matter? Call and ask. Express your heart to him. God will read the caller ID and read your intent immediately. Words do matter. He's given his Word, and it's important to give yours. Here's an example of the kinds of words you can use in an exchange with God. What have you to lose but everything you can't carry yourself? Repeat the following words verbatim if it helps. Or take the gist and say it in your own way:

> Jesus, I've made poor choices that have hurt others and myself. I've done deeds that have created damaging outcomes. I've avoided other things that would have bettered the world and my own soul. I've left my mark, and it hasn't been all positive. I'm responsible for these actions and inactions. When the accounts of the universe

are balanced, I will stand bankrupt. Try as I might, I will never succeed in clearing my name. I need your help. You have offered to take my debt, to bear my Karma, and give me in exchange the consequences of your perfect life. I accept this gracious offer. I give you my life and receive in return your virtue. You accept me; I accept you. Come and live your life through me.

Done. The exchange is real and complete. And yet it doesn't remain a static event. The exchange of your life for Jesus' life is not a mechanical formula but an invitation into a dynamic relationship—with a living Person. This means, practically, that I can, at any moment, as I move through my days, pause and reaffirm this agreement. When I screw up and know the consequences from some action I've perpetrated will soon fall upon me, I can give them to Jesus and take in return his goodness. This is no magical "out" from bearing any and every consequence of my choices. If I rob a bank and get caught, Jesus isn't going to serve my sentence in prison. It does mean I can daily, moment by moment, shift my moral obligation to him and be free in my spirit even when and if society or nature must inflict their due upon me.

Simply put, Karma exchange can become my lifestyle, like breathing in and out, receiving Jesus' goodness, giving him my "less-than" goodness, while I drive to work, walk the dog, eat lunch, lie down to sleep, rise to face a new day. "I give you my life; I receive yours."

Again, the Karma of Jesus . . .

- I reap what I sow—Karma.
- I sow trouble; I get trouble.

- If someone lived a perfect life would they have perfect Karma?
- Jesus lived a perfect life.
- He offers to exchange lives with me.
- He takes my trouble—my Karma.
- He gives me his consequences—his Karma. I can accept his offer.

> Explore this further at *www.DumpYourKarma.com* and *www.KarmaOfJesus.com*.

Bad news came on Thursday, April 17, 2008. My father died. The dread of his departure had hung over our heads for weeks, like an anvil tied to a fraying rope. Still the full weight of sorrow did not snap and crush me until I heard the words "He's gone."

In the weeks immediately following my encounter with Andrew, my father recovered remarkably well from the damage caused by the initial hemorrhage. We dared hope for the best. He talked and walked some. His mischievous, teasing humor returned with a special gentleness added in. The rehab center told us they planned to discharge him on Friday the eighteenth.

When I visited him Wednesday night I sensed something fading in him. He sat in a kind of blissful daze, utterly delightful and delighted, and full of charm and playful sweetness, but he seemed to me like an impressionist's painting—blurred around the edges, yet packed with meaning. His spirit grew as his body shut down. We sat together. We said little. I brought him an advance copy of my first book, which had just come in the mail the day before. He held it with more reverence than it deserved and smiled. I knew he felt proud. I felt sorrow.

Three hours after I left him, he fell asleep for the last time.

Yes, I believe that things happen for a reason and that bad news has to come before the good news. I'm counting on that as I count on this new chance for a fresh start, a life now with all the benefits of true personal liberty and friendship with the One who knows you best and loves you most. My Designer and Maker paid the price for the privilege of walking with you into a great destiny that begins now and lasts forever.

NOTES

CHAPTER 1: KARMA-ISH

page 17   This conversation with a young man I call "Andrew" really happened, and it did set off the dominoes that eventually resulted in this book. I've changed Andrew's name for two reasons. First, I want to protect the confidential nature of our discussions. Second, Andrew is really *two* people, and what I represent in this book as one conversation actually comprises two distinct encounters with individuals who do not know one another but engaged me with similar questions and opinions. I've compiled the essence and content of both dialogues into one scene, which happened as I describe it here. "Andrew I"—the young man who actually did heckle me—disappeared out of my life the night I met and talked with him. "Andrew II" remains a friend. We meet periodically to carry on our discussions of life and God.

CHAPTER 2: THE GIFT OF THE MAGI?

page 25   While the detailed belief system of the ancient magi remains a mystery, *The Catholic Encyclopedia* (*www.catholic.org/ encyclopedia/view.php?id=6650*) offers a basic outline of their philosophy.

page 25   "Karma . . . means 'action and the action-influence' ": The *Encyclopedia of Religion* defines Karma as ". . . the dynamic manifestation of mental and physical energy in deeds, speech, or thought inevitably producing the good, evil, or neutral effect, either immediately, or in the future. . . . The effect itself becomes the cause of further effect, making the self in the case of the individual, a process of unceasing transformation from one life to another in the wheel of transmigration, and the world, in the case of the universe, a process of perpetual becoming." Vergilius Firm, *Encyclopedia of Religion* (New York: Philosophical Library, Inc., 1945), "Karma," 101.

page 26   Emerson's essay "Compensation" brilliantly encapsulates the belief that the universe is its own equalizer. It's available at *www.vcu.edu/engweb/transcendentalism/authors/emerson/essays/compensation.html.*

page 27   The *Bhagavad Gita* is available in its entirety at *www.bhagavad-gita.org.*

page 28   "This Hindu tradition identifies Karma in three forms": H. L. Richard has worked in India for decades, articulating the Christian spiritual tradition in a Hindu context. His books offer a credible bridge of understanding between cultures. His succinct definition of the complexity of Hindu Karma is most helpful. H. L. Richard, *Exploring the Depths of the Mystery of Christ* (Bangalore, India: Center for Contemporary Christianity, 2005), introduction.

page 29   "Around 490 BCE, a savior appeared in Kapilavastu: the child Gautama": *The Catholic Encyclopedia* offers a succinct description of the early history of Buddhism as well as the foundational philosophical beliefs of the religion: *www.newadvent.org/cathen/03028b.htm.*

page 30   "Nemesis evened the score": The Greek pantheon personified the philosophy of universal "compensation" in the goddesses Ananke and Nemesis: *www.theoi.com/Protogenos/Ananke.html* and *www.theoi.com/Daimon/Nemesis.html.*

page 31   "One single 'theory of everything,' recognized by the Hindu word *Karma*, grew to maturity almost simultaneously in two distinct . . . civilizations": Thomas McEvilley explores the mysterious connection between ancient Greek and ancient Hindu thought. He notes the remarkable parallels between Plato's version of reincarnation and what developed in India. Like many historians, he struggles to successfully explain this connection. Thomas McEvilley, *The Shape of Ancient Thought* (New York: Allworth Press, 2002), 1st edition, 108.

page 32 "possible Karma parallels in the Jewish and Christian traditions": Mark 4:24–25, Holy Bible, New International Version (Grand Rapids, MI: Zondervan, 2005); Galatians 6:7; Matthew 7:1–2; Hosea 8:7; Job 4:8; Exodus 21:23–25; Numbers 32:23, Holy Bible, New Living Translation (Wheaton, IL: Tyndale House, 2004).

page 34 "No harm comes to the godly": Proverbs 12:21; Proverbs 13:21; Proverbs 15:6, Holy Bible, New Living Translation.

page 36 "Was Karma the first gift of the magi?": The champion of this theory is M. L. West in his *Early Greek Philosophy and the Orient* (New York: Oxford University Press, USA, 1971, 2001), 242. West contends that the magi were monists and believed in the transmigration of the soul in reincarnation based on a person's moral behavior. West's theory is that the magi spread this vision when they scattered east and west. West believes that the magi helped solidify and articulate these ideas in both India and Greece. McEvilley (see above) disputes West's thesis, pointing out what he says are problems with West's dates and questioning whether the magi were in fact monists.

page 37 "the Jutaka": Thomas McEvilley references this poem in *The Shape of Ancient Thought*, 1st edition, 140.

page 37 "this magus . . . noticed the first of a series of phenomena that he and others took as a significant sign": This fascinating account of the magian journey to find Jesus is told by astronomer Frederick Larson at *www.bethlehemstar.net/*.

CHAPTER 3: GUILT BY ASSOCIATION

page 43 A more thorough summary of what sparked World War I is found at Henry F. Klein, *The Encyclopedia Americana,* Volume XXVIII, "European War" (New York: Encyclopedia Americana Corporation, 1920), 268.

page 44   "a sociological theory known as 'broken windows' ": Chantal
            Britt, "Broken Windows' Crime Theory Explains Graffiti
            Mailbox Thieves," www.bloomberg.com/apps/news?pid=206011
            03&sid=aC8SCcalyOBc&refer=us.

page 51   "War of the Worlds radio broadcast": One account of Welles'
            spoof/fiasco is relayed at http://history1900s.about
            .com/od/1930s/a/warofworlds_2.htm.

page 52   The impact of wolves on Yellowstone's ecological balance is
            detailed in an article posted at www.yellowstonenationalpark
            .com/wolves.htm.

page 54   "James Gleick's watershed book": Chaos: Making a New Sci-
            ence (New York: Penguin Books, 1988), 23.

page 56   "This is perplexing": Ravi Zacharias, The Lotus and the Cross:
            Jesus Talks With Buddha (Sisters, OR: Multnomah, 2001),
            chapter 1.

page 58   "I don't want to do what is wrong, but I do it anyway":
            Romans 7:19, Holy Bible, New Living Translation.

CHAPTER 4: SCAMMING THE SYSTEM

page 61   "The first book I swiped changed my life forever": E. Stanley
            Jones, Christ at the Round Table (New York: Abingdon Press,
            1928).

page 61   "Ari Derfel . . . stored all his personal waste inside his Berke-
            ley, California, apartment": Kelly Zito, "It's No Garbage
            Strike: Man Keeps a Year's Worth of Trash," www.sfgate.com/
            cgi-bin/object/article?f=/c/a/2007/12/30/BAFFU493E.DTL&o=0.

page 63   "Giacomo Puccini, the great composer of operas": Richard
            Specht and Catherine Alison Phillips, Giacomo Puccini: The
            Man, His Life, His Work, Catherine Alison Phillips, trans.
            (New York: Knopf, 1933), 32.

page 63   "the Madoff financial scandal": Robert Lenzner, "Bernie Mad-
            off's $50 Billion Ponzi Scheme," www.forbes.com/2008/12/12/
            madoff-ponzi-hedge-pf-ii-in_rl_1212croesus_inl.html.

page 65   "Anthony Robbins": For a summary description of Anthony Robbins' seminars, see *www.tonyrobbins-seminar.com/upw_ summary.html.*

page 67   "Gino Castignoli . . . [and] his beloved Red Sox": Angela Montefinise, Brad Hamilton, Alex Ginsberg, and James Fanelli, "Hammering the Hex: Stadium Hardhats Uncover Sox Shirt," *www.nypost.com/seven/04132008/news/regional news/hammering_the_hex_106315.htm.*

page 67   "A researcher in England": Richard Wiseman's findings on "good luck" practices are outlined at *www.richardwiseman .com/research/superstition.html.*

page 68   "Eckhart Tolle": For a summary description of Eckhart Tolle's teachings see *www.eckharttolle.com/eckharttolle-about.*

page 69   "most resolutions don't work": There has been a great deal of research conducted on the phenomenon of resolutions. For a review, see John Grohol, "The Psychology of New Year's Resolutions," *http://psychcentral.com/blog/ archives/2008/12/28/the-psychology-of-new-years-resolutions/.*

page 69   "Macbeth": See William Shakespeare, *Macbeth*, Act 5, scene 1, 26–40.

page 71   "I have discovered this principle of life": Romans 7:21–24, Holy Bible, New Living Translation.

page 72   James Leroy Scott's attempted escape: This story ran on WCCO.com, July 24, 2008, *http://wcco.com/crime/prison.escape .planned.2.778789.html.*

CHAPTER 5: WEB OF INTRIGUE

page 79   The Mount Hood story ran on June 1, 2002. It's posted at *www.i-world.net/oma/news/accidents/2002-05-30-hood.html.*

page 80   Maureen Naylor, "Fog, Speed & Drunk Driver Contributed to 100-Vehicle Pileup," *http://abclocal.go.com/kfsn/ story?section=news/local&id=5740322.*

page 80   "The crowd of would-be Wal-Mart bargain hunters": Robert
             D. McFadden and Angela Macropoulos, "Wal-Mart Employee
             Trampled to Death," *www.nytimes.com/2008/11/29/*
             business/29walmart.html.

page 82   "You must not make for yourself an idol": Exodus 20:4–6,
             Holy Bible, New Living Translation.

page 83   "The parents have eaten sour grapes": Jeremiah 31:29, Holy
             Bible, New Living Translation.

page 84   "Some Buddhist teaching about Karma includes a clause
             called 'transfer of merit' ": This idea is outlined in an article
             by T. W. Rhys Davids, *The Encyclopedia of Religion and Ethics,*
             Part 10, "Expiation and Atonement: Hindu," James Hastings,
             ed. (Whitefish, MT: Kessinger Publishing, 2003), 641. It is
             also explained by Esban Andreasen, *Popular Buddhism in Japan*
             (Honolulu, HI: University of Hawaii Press, 1997), 61.

page 85   "treasury of merit": This Catholic doctrine is explained at
             www.newadvent.org/cathen/10202b.htm.

page 85   *Shoeless Joe,* later adapted into the film *Field of Dreams,* was
             written by W. P. Kinsella (Boston: Houghton Mifflin, 1982).

page 86   *War and Peace,* by Leo Tolstoy (New York: Vintage Classics,
             1869, 2008), was first published 140 years ago.

page 87   *Crime and Punishment,* by Fyodor Dostoevsky (New York:
             Bantam Classics, 1866, 1996), was published just three years
             before *War and Peace.*

page 87   "The Wish House," Rudyard Kipling's short story, was first
             published in *MacLean's Magazine* (October 1924). See *www*
             .kipling.org.uk/rg_wishouse1.htm for notes on the story.

page 88   *Descent Into Hell,* by Charles Williams, was published in 1949
             (Grand Rapids, MI: Eerdmans).

page 90   "This was a power which [C. S.] Lewis found himself later to
             possess": From Walter Hooper, *C. S. Lewis: A Companion and*
             Guide (New York: HarperCollins, 1996), 85.

page 92   "Covenant" is explained in F. C. Finsham, *The International Standard Bible Encyclopedia A–D*, "Covenant," Geoffrey W. Bromiley, ed. (Grand Rapids, MI: Eerdmans, 1995), 790–92.

CHAPTER 6: A WORMHOLE INTO ETERNITY

page 99   "forensic scientists . . . built a composite of a face they claim represents a typical thirty-year-old male of Jesus' time and place": This rendering ran in *Popular Mechanics* (December 2002). Mike Fillon, "Real Face of Jesus," *www.popularmechanics.com/science/research/1282186.html*.

page 101   "Gumbel makes a succinct argument for the reliability of the accounts of Jesus' life": Nicky Gumbel, *Questions of Life* (Colorado Springs: Cook, 1993), 25.

page 112   *A Tale of Two Cities* (New York: Penguin Classics edition, 2003) was originally published in 1859 in sections in a new magazine Charles Dickens created called *All the Year Round*.

page 113   *The Four Loves*, by C. S. Lewis, was first published in 1960.

page 117   "For God so loved the world": John 3:16, Holy Bible, New International Version.

CHAPTER 7: CHRIST SUBMERGED

page 123   "Father, forgive those who have done this to me": This is my paraphrase of Luke 23:34 from the Holy Bible. Accounts of Jesus' crucifixion are given in each of the Gospels: Matthew, Mark, Luke, and John.

page 123   "Today you will come with me to a safe and splendid place": My paraphrase of Luke 23:43.

page 123   "John, please care for her": My paraphrase of John 19:26–27.

page 123   "My God, my God, why have you deserted me to this?": My paraphrase of Matthew 27:46.

page 123   "It is finished! Father": My paraphrase of John 19:30.

page 124   "Jesus died on a Friday afternoon": Information about Jesus
                can also be found in Nicky Gumbel's book *Questions of Life*, 48.

page 128   "theories of atonement": Explanations of the various theo-
                ries of Christian atonement can be found in many reviews,
                such as the following article in Stanford University's *Stan-
                ford Philosophy Encyclopedia*. *http://plato.stanford.edu/entries/
                christiantheology-philosophy/#Ato*, "Philosophy and Christian
                Theology."

page 129   Maximilian Kolbe's story can be explored at *www.fatherkolbe
                .com*.

page 132   "Light is a wave and a particle": These amateur specula-
                tions into the realms of physics are fascinating to con-
                template, though certainly not solid science. For a better
                grounding, check out more established sources, such as
                http://physicsworld.com/cws/article/news/2815.

page 138   "This is what we are doing to Christ": Wendy Beckett's
                comments about Andres Serrano's photograph *Piss Christ* are
                recorded in an article: Eleanor Heartney, "A Consecrated
                Critic," *Art in America* (July 1998).

page 139   "*The Dark Knight*": Christopher Nolan's film has grossed over
                $1 billion in worldwide distribution.

page 140   "There was nothing beautiful or majestic about his appear-
                ance": Isaiah 53:2–5, Holy Bible, New Living Translation.

CHAPTER 8: TAKING EVERYTHING PERSONALLY

page 146   "In *Christ at the Round Table*, Jones recalls": E. Stanley Jones,
                Christ at the Round Table, 67–69.

page 148   Abraham Lincoln's Second Inaugural Address can be found
                in the National Archive, *www.loc.gov/rr/program/bib/ourdocs/
                Lincoln2nd.html*.

page 150   Judge Roy Bean's story can be explored at *www.legends
                ofamerica.com/law-roybean.html*.

page 152   "God is greater. Glory be to thee, O God, and praise": This is a classic Muslim prayer. See George Appleton, ed., *The Oxford Book of Prayer* (New York: Oxford University Press, 1985), 336.

page 155   "*Fiddler on the Roof*": This Broadway musical, which opened in 1964, was written by Joseph Stein, with lyrics by Sheldon Harnick and music by Jerry Bock. It is based on a Yiddish book published in 1894 titled *Tevye and His Daughters* (or *Tevye the Milkman*) and other tales by Sholem Aleichem. The script can be read at *www.script-o-rama.com/movie_scripts/f/fiddler-on-the-roof-script.html*.

page 156   "The thing I mean can be seen . . . in children": G. K. Chesterton, *Orthodoxy* (New York: Image Books, 1959), 60.

page 157   "Be audacious with God": My paraphrase of Luke 11:5–13.

page 158   "Keep on asking, and you will receive what you ask for": Matthew 7:7–8, Holy Bible, New Living Translation.

page 158   "a study done by a medical doctor named Randolph Byrd": R. B. Byrd, "Positive therapeutic effects of intercessory prayer in a coronary care unit population," *Southern Medical Journal*, 81 (1988): 826–29.

page 159   "the students we prayed for secretly were three times more likely to say they wouldn't smoke": Mark Herringshaw, *The Effect of Long-Distance Intercessory Prayer and Anti-Smoking Communication on Teenagers' Intention to Smoke Cigarettes*, PhD dissertation for Regent University, Center for Leadership Studies (2001).

CHAPTER 9: TO BOOT

page 165   "Assayas: . . . I am beginning to understand religion": From Michka Assayas, *Bono: In Conversation with Michka Assayas* (New York: Riverhead Books, 2005), 225, 227.

page 167   "As E. Stanley Jones put it": Jones, *Christ at the Round Table*, 94.

page 170   "I no longer live, but Christ lives in me": Galatians 2:20, Holy Bible, New International Version.

page 178   "As the apostle Paul once put it, 'I want to know Christ' ":
Philippians 3:10, Holy Bible, New International Version.

CHAPTER 10: COMING CLEAN

page 181   John Fraiser's insights into Johnny Cash's music can be found
on his blog at *http://chaosandoldnight.wordpress.com/2007/12/06/
the-law-and-gospel-according-to-johnny-cash/*.

page 188   "The story of a curious young man who peppers Jesus with
questions": My paraphrase of Mark 10:17–25.

page 188   "Jesus tells another story of a wealthy father": My paraphrase of Luke 15:11–32.

page 190   The story of David and Nathan can be found in 2 Samuel
12:1–11.

page 191   "Have mercy on me, O God": Psalm 51:1–4, Holy Bible,
New Living Translation.

ABOUT THE AUTHOR

Mark Herringshaw, PhD, currently serves as a teaching pastor at the 7,000-member North Heights Lutheran Church in St. Paul, Minnesota. A conference speaker and seminary professor, Mark is known for leveraging the crafts of storytelling, biblical scholarship, and scientific research to make complex ideas simple, practical, and transformative. Mark has done graduate work at Luther Seminary and Regent College and holds a PhD in leadership from Regent University. He and his wife, Jill, have four children and make their home near St. Paul.